INNER WILD

MUSINGS IN EXPRESSIVE ARTS THERAPY AND ECOPSYCHOLOGY

NICKI KOETHNER & SURAYA KEATING

Copyright © 2025 NICKI KOETHNER & SURAYA KEATING

All rights reserved

First Edition

"Trees are the poems that the earth writes upon the sky."
Kahlil Gibran

TABLE OF CONTENTS

PART 1: CHILDREN AS TEACHERS OF THE WILD 1
    MY SON AND THE TREES 6
    Rain Elizabeth Stickney

PART 2: EXPLORATIONS 9
    COMING BACK HOME TO THE WILD SELF 10
    Marcela Sabin
    WILD WOMAN PHOTOSHOOT 19
    Abby Kojola
    ALLOWING CREATIVE INSPIRATION FROM
    OUR NATURAL ENVIRONMENTS 27
    Anin Utigaard
    EXPANDING ATTACHMENT THEORY: THE
    ARMS OF INFINITY AND BEYOND 34
    Martha Hines
    EARTH, THE SOUL, AND THE CREATIVE
    IMPULSE: A LIFE LED ON PURPOSE 40
    Jo Burrows
    ECOUTEARTH 49
    Karina Colliat
    INTO THE WILD: THE DANCE OF EGO AND SOUL .55
    Nicki Koethner
    I CHOOSE FREEDOM 59
    Suraya Susana Keating

PART 3: POETRY OF THE WILD 64

SAMILA – FROM SHAME TO BEAUTY 65
Mireya Alejo Marcet

JOURNEY TO DEEP SOVEREIGNTY 70
Aimee Tomczak

THE ESSENCE OF MY SOUL 74
Nicki Koethner

MESSAGE FROM WATER 76
Suraya Susana Keating

PART 4: VOICES OF THE ELDERS 79

UNEARTHING THE UNDERWORLD WOMB TEMPLE 81
Kerani Marie

GOING OUT AND RETURNING WITH MY GIFTS FOR MY PEOPLE 85
Sharon Reinbott

REFLECTIONS 88
Saunterre Irish

PART 5: PRACTICES 90

EARTH PRACTICES 91
WATER PRACTICES 97
FIRE PRACTICES 100
AIR PRACTICES 103
MIXED ELEMENTS PRACTICES 106

FOREWORD

This book is a gathering of voices, experiences, and practices from expressive arts and ecopsychology, inviting you to reconnect with your wild soul. Through writings, personal stories, creative exercises, and artistic expressions, we offer pathways to deepen your connection with nature and yourself.

We hope to inspire you—to play in the dirt, embody the elements, sing with the birds, paint and dance what is alive in your heart, walk barefoot, and lie on the Earth to listen. Blending poetry, quotes, images, and practical suggestions, this book serves as both a mirror and a guide, reminding you of the wildness within.

Feeling called to explore this theme, we invited friends and colleagues to reflect on "Embracing Your Inner Wild." Their diverse perspectives weave a tapestry of interconnectedness, reinforcing the ancient wisdom that lives within us. In a world shaped by capitalism and disconnection, where anxiety, depression, and isolation are widespread, this book seeks to restore balance—reminding us that we are not separate from nature; we *are* nature.

Soul, the Wild, and Ancient Wisdom

Soul moves through us like wind through the trees. It speaks in infinite ways, just as nature expresses herself through every being, element, and energy. Soul connects us to the vast mystery of existence, beyond what logic and research can fully grasp.

We acknowledge that what we *don't* know far exceeds what we *do* know. When we cling too tightly to certainty, we risk missing the truth of the moment. In embracing the unknown, we cultivate wonder—raw, unbound, and full of possibility. We let go of assumptions and invoke a beginner's mind, seeing the world with the curiosity of a child. Regardless of age, this sacred innocence remains within us, waiting to be remembered.

We invite you to express the wildness of your emotions, to dissolve into your elemental nature, and to shift from overthinking into embodied presence. The true evidence of this journey lies in our well-being, in our deepening relationship with beauty, abundance, and the life force that sustains us all.

Ancient wisdom teaches that we are made of the elements, and they are part of us. Yet, modern life has distanced us from this truth. This book is an invitation to restore balance, honor our innate knowing, and reclaim our connection to soul, nature, and all that is.

We invite you to be with and express the wildness of your emotions.

Dissolving into our elemental essential natures helps us to access our senses and felt experience rather than our thoughts, judgments, and concepts about our experience. It helps us to move into our bodies and away from our thinking mind.

The evidence we are seeking is in our well-being and connection to the beauty, bounty, and abundance of the universe. We are reconnecting our life force with the larger life force of the universe and thus re-establishing the natural reciprocity that exists between all living beings.

Ancient wisdom tells us we are part of the elements, and the elements are part of us. The separation that we have all experienced in different forms has disconnected us from our wild selves. This book is an invitation to re-balance the way we live and to honor that deeper knowing that connects us back to our soul, to the elements, and to all that is.

Expressive Arts, Creativity and Connecting with Soul

As artists, expressive arts therapists, and editors of this book, we felt called to gather a community of voices to share reflections and practices that illuminate the power of creativity, nature, and the arts as gateways to the wild soul.

May this book serve as an invitation—to listen, to feel, to create, and to remember who you truly are.

What is Expressive Arts Therapy?

Expressive Arts Therapy is a multimodal therapeutic approach to healing and growth that emerged in a more formal way in the mid-twentieth century and has blossomed in a more expansive way in the twenty-first century. The field of Expressive Arts Therapy was first established by Lesley University professors Shaun McNiff, Paolo Knill and others in the early 1970's. Natalie Rogers is another pioneer in the field. She integrated the expressive arts into the work of her father, Carl Roger, founder of the Person-Centered Approach. See Anin Utigaard's writing for more information. The International Expressive Arts Therapy Association (IEATA) is a non-profit organization founded in 1994. It aims to encourage the "creative spirit" and supports expressive arts therapists, artists, educators, consultants, and others using integrative, multi-modal arts processes for personal and community growth. IEATA provides a professional guild and an international network through sponsoring bi-annual conferences. It provides a global forum for dialogue, promotes guiding principles for professional practice, and works to increase recognition and use of expressive arts as a tool for psychological, physical and spiritual wellness. IEATA offers two kinds of registration for professional memberships, REAT and REACE. See more info on www.ieata.org.

Expressive Arts Therapy has ancient roots. People around the world in multiple cultures have engaged in music, art-making, craft-making, theater and poetry since the beginning of time. Shamans and medicine people have utilized drumming, chanting, sound, dancing, and dramatic enactment for healing of their communities and individuals. Creative expression as a gateway to self-awareness, healing, growth, wisdom, spirituality, and the embodied expression of our aliveness existed since the beginning of time.

Some of the key tenets of Expressive Arts Therapy that we consider valuable are as follows:

- Creativity is inherent in all beings. We are all creative and we are all creators.
- What is most important in art-making (whether it is visual art, music, movement, theater or another medium) is the *process* and not the *product*.
- Various forms of expression are used together to enhance one another and deepen the process of connecting with the soul. Engaging in one arts modality can inspire creative expression in another modality. For example, dancing can inspire painting. Visual art can inspire creative writing, and we can sound and move our paintings as well as create music in response to a movement or vice-versa etc.

Creativity, which pours through all of us, plays a crucial role in connecting us to our soul, and is a much-needed medicine in these times during which the modernization of our lives often jeopardizes our connection to nature, to our organic inner rhythms, to the wild.

This book is not a therapy book but a guide for living from our soul, for walking the path that is authentic to us, and for embracing with full abandon the beautiful, messy, unpredictable, sacred path of the wild. We play with our innate creative nature to loosen rigid structures and discover ourselves anew.

Creativity serves as a bridge between the soul and the body, deepening our connection to the senses and opening pathways to alternative ways of knowing—beyond the confines of logic. In dreams, this unfolds naturally, as the judging mind—our ego, shaped by internalized expectations of "shoulds" and "musts"—rests, allowing the soul to express itself freely.

Creative expression is the language of the soul and inherent in all of us. Many adults feel they can't sing, draw, or dance, yet as children these expressions were a natural form of language for them. Due to the experience of external judgments, critical comments and a constant process of being evaluated while growing up, the gateway to the soul of some people becomes shut down, blocking expression in different areas of their lives. It also opens us to grieve and access emotions that were repressed due to reactions we received while growing up.

When we utilize creative expression in a process-oriented way rather than being focused on the product as many of us have been taught in schools, we promote a body and heart knowing, enhancing our inner guidance system and intuition. Inner critic voices might come up in the process of reconnecting with ourselves and our bodies, such as "am *I doing it right?*" "*I can't sing, move, draw*" ..."*I'm not a visual artist*" and other conditioned voices that have separated us from a deeper sense of connection with ourselves. These internalized critical voices have originated from experiences in our childhood when we were criticized, judged and reacted to by our environment and then reinforced by societal norms of conditioning and schooling.

Creativity helps us to access the gift of our uniqueness and can support our sense of belonging to the earth and cosmos. Being in the creative process allows us to be present to what is emerging in the moment and see what movement might want to happen in response to inner impulses and outer stimuli. Creating images, for example, can build a bridge to our inner worlds otherwise hidden, even to ourselves. Sounding and singing, playing instruments can shift inner states and thought processes, harmonizing frequencies within our bodies and connecting us with a field that is larger than our logical knowing and understanding. Dancing and moving freely can support the healthy flow and release of emotions. Drama can help us access and express parts of ourselves that we may otherwise be afraid of or ashamed to express.

We might encounter fears that have made it feel unsafe to be connected to our interior worlds and bodies in the process as well. Staying with the process and/or having a guide in these processes can shift the blockages these voices and fears have created and transform stuck energy while supporting the containment, integration and digestion of traumatic or other upsetting experiences. It can also open us to feeling emotions that have been repressed and access our personal and collective grief to events in the present and past.

Expressive arts reopen the gateway to the soul thus freeing us from an external locus of control to an internal process of being, inviting us to have our authentic voices be the guiding force in our lives.

We hope that you find the contributions to this book inspiring in evoking your own creativity and well-being, and to grieve whatever needs grieving. In doing so, we aim to support the well-being of the larger collective to bring peace, justice, balance and joy to this world.

Suraya Keating and Nicki Koethner, Fairfax, CA 2025

Part 1

CHILDREN AS TEACHERS OF THE WILD

Our friend Sefora's son shared this with her spontaneously on a walk:

*"I love the mountain with the water mama,"
he says, referring to the waterfall.*

INTRODUCTION
Nicki Koethner

Children exist closer to the source of our interdependence—fully embodied, attuned to the wider energetic field of existence. They have not yet been conditioned to live solely in their minds, disconnected from their bodies. Instead, they remain instinctively tethered to the wild, moving in rhythm with the natural world.

The freshness of their perception, the effortless connection they share with nature, is palpable in the stories and quotes that follow. In many ways, children become our teachers, reminding us of what truly matters. They invite us to return—to presence, to simplicity, to a more vivid, wholehearted way of living.

The following stories about some experiences I have had with children remind me of:

- The deeper, intrinsic knowing of our interdependence.
- The transformative power of the arts in guiding the soul through pain and emotional challenges.
- The role of creative expression in helping us navigate separation anxiety, loneliness, impermanence, and death.

Many years ago, I was babysitting a three-year-old boy. That morning, his father and sister had already left for work, and when his mother said goodbye, he began to cry. Comforting him with hugs and soothing words proved challenging, his sadness ran deep.

Gently, I invited him outside into the garden. He gravitated toward an easel and finger paints, his small frame still trembling with soft sobs as I held space for him. Then, without prompting, he began to paint. I stood back, watching as he instinctively chose colors, his emotions pouring onto the canvas. Slowly, his sobbing quieted.

When his painting was complete, he set it aside and ventured further into the garden, playing with his toys, his energy lighter. Before long, he turned to me, engaging with a newfound ease. I was mesmerized. Without direction, without instruction, he had known exactly what he needed, his own form of healing, expressed through art.

On another occasion, I cared for a diverse group of five toddlers, ages three to four, each from different cultural backgrounds. One afternoon, as they gathered for lunch, two of the boys began playing together. One pretended to shoot the other, mimicking a gesture he had likely seen before.

Without hesitation, the other boy responded, his voice filled with raw, childlike wisdom: "Don't shoot me. I just came out of my mother's belly!"

His words struck me. So simple, yet profound. This moment was a reminder of the deep knowing and intuition that we are all born with an unspoken awareness that connects us to the essence of life itself.

One day, while caring for a four-year-old girl, she became fascinated by my necklace, which bore an Om symbol. Curious, she traced it with her small fingers and asked what it meant.

"Om is the sound of the universe," I explained.

She tilted her head, intrigued. "What's the universe?"

Smiling, I answered, "The universe is you, me, your parents, the stars, the sun, the trees, the animals, and all the plants."

As I spoke, her eyes grew wider and wider, taking in the vastness of what I had described. Then, after a moment of silence, she turned to her mother and snuggled in closer. "I want my mommy," she whispered.

Her reaction surprised me at first, but then I understood—what I had described felt too immense, too boundless. In that moment, she needed something familiar, something grounding. She needed her mother's presence to remind her that even in the vastness of the universe, she was not alone.

The last story brings me back to my own experience of confronting death and impermanence as a child. I was nine years old, lying in bed, overcome with tears as I imagined the inevitable—one day, my parents and brothers would be gone. And what would happen to me? The thought was unbearable.

My mother sat beside me, trying to soothe me, but my sobs wouldn't stop. Finally, she said gently, "Your dad can explain it better."

When my father came in, he spoke calmly, his voice steady. "It is only our body that dies. Our soul continues to live." And just like that, my crying stopped.

The moment he said it, something inside me shifted. I didn't fully understand what the soul was—not in a way my mind could grasp. But something deeper in me remembered.

A STORY FROM A 5-YEAR-OLD

The following example shows one way to support children to keep their access to a deeper knowing and to creativity alive. The story was created by a five-year-old responding to images given to him, and his mother recorded the story.

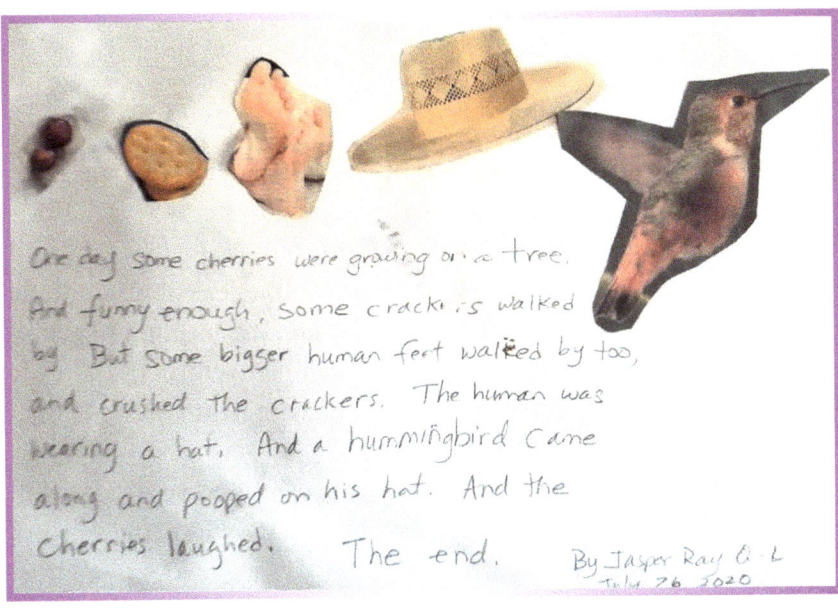

One day some cherries were growing on a tree. And funny enough, some crackers walked by. But some bigger human feet walked by too, and crushed the crackers. The human was wearing a hat. And a hummingbird came along and pooped on his hat. And the cherries laughed. The end. By Jasper Ray O-L July 26 2020

This is a playful way of engaging the imagination that children have natural access to. By not asking a child to make logical sense out of something, their natural creativity is kept alive. Following the liminal space of creation is something that adults have to relearn after years of schooling. The power of imagination and creativity is essential across the life-span to respond to life's challenges and engage in a full range of possibilities.

MY SON AND THE TREES
Rain Elizabeth Stickney

I intentionally allow my son to find his own path in the spiritual, psychic, and religious realms. I do not presume to know what his life holds for him, but I trust his journey completely.

At the time of this story, he was nine years old. His understanding of the world was just beginning to unfold, and it continues to evolve as he moves through the time-space of his life. Even then, I already knew he was deeply spiritual I had recognized his innate connection to the sacred from the very beginning.

There are moments when my son comes to me, eyes bright with wonder, eager to share his experiences—glimpses into the unseen, reflections of something greater.

One winter day, as we were sledding, I watched him wander over to a beautiful tree. A gentle thought passed through my mind: *Oh, that's so nice. He's with the tree.* That was all. A quiet contentment settled inside me. It was simply a precious moment to witness.

Later that day, he came to me, his voice filled with quiet certainty. "Mommy, I can hear the tree talk to me… and I can talk to the tree."

A resonance grew between us as he spoke, his small hands gesturing to show how he had touched the tree, felt its energy, and listened. He described the silent conversation, an unspoken language exchanged through an inward channel of connection.

Warmth spread through me, a quiet thrill rising in my chest. He knew—he *understood* something I had always known too. Nature is alive, filled with beings, each with a voice of its own. Trees, like old friends, speak to us if we are willing to listen. And we, in turn, can be in conscious relationship with them.

Even now, I remain an honored witness to his unfolding discovery. As he communes with nature in his own way, I get to walk alongside him—marveling at the depth of his connection, the unspoken wisdom he carries, and the endless conversations waiting to be heard.

BIOGRAPHY

Rain is a healer and meditation teacher in private practice. Originally from the San Francisco Bay Area, she now lives in Vermont on wild, forested land with her son, life partner, and their magical bunny.

She holds a Bachelor's degree in Psychology with specialized studies in Biofeedback and Somatics, as well as a Master's degree in East-West Psychology with a Certificate in Expressive Arts Consulting and Education. Trained in Hand in Hand Parenting by Connection and The Gottman Method—both trauma-informed approaches—Rain integrates these modalities into her work to support healing with mindfulness, depth, and compassion. With a background in bodywork spanning two decades, she developed her own approach, Emotional Integrative Bodywork, which honors the four pillars of human experience: body, mind, heart, and spirit.

Rain is also the host of the podcast Every Moment Is Sacred, where she explores the interweaving of healing and meditation into everyday life.

HEART OF THE TREE BY: 6-YEAR-OLD LYRA

Jason, Lyra's father says: *When my daughter Lyra made this image for me, its message was so moving that I teared up. My career has been focused around trees -- striving through many ups and downs to advance environmentally and socially responsible management of working forests and to protect and restore those that should not be used for timber production. Lyra gave this to me when I was at a low point in my career: I did not have enough work, and was frustrated and tired of struggling to find ways to make enough money to make it. This message illuminated my heart and reminded me that this is my life's work, a big part of what gives it purpose and meaning, and that I needed to stick with it because it was not "broken." In fact, it was only "hidden away in the heart of the tree."*

PART 2

EXPLORATIONS

GUIDING QUESTIONS FOR OUR WRITERS IN THIS SECTION INCLUDE:

- What is the wild to you?
- How has art inspired you?
- How do you connect with your soul?
- When has life touched or inspired the wild in you?

COMING BACK HOME TO THE WILD SELF

Marcela Sabin

What is the wild to you?

As I search for the meaning of *wild*, countless definitions arise. But for me, the wild self is an intimate connection to our true essence, our longings, passions, and the raw, untamed truth of who we are. It is the freedom to exist unapologetically, where reverence and curiosity intertwine, where the sacred and the mundane merge into one.

How has art inspired you?

I confess, my inner wildness does not always reveal itself. It needs a safe container, a space where it can unfold without fear. It is still a work in progress, an evolving force within me.

How do you connect with your soul?

When I think of the wild, an image comes to mind of life flourishing in places untouched by human hands. In the depths of the forest, plants grow in exuberant harmony, weaving a dance of survival and beauty. Wild animals move with an effortless rhythm, shifting between stillness and raw, potent energy. There is no hesitation, no need for permission, only the instinctual pulse of life, unrestrained and free.

When has life touched the wild in me?

I can still recall moments when I surrendered completely to the flow of energy while dancing—where nothing else mattered. The intensity of becoming a channel for that energy, the exhaustion creeping into my limbs—it was all irrelevant in the face of pure ecstasy.

The wild also reminds me of making love—a fusion of instinct and transcendence, a meeting of earth and sky. Yet one of the most powerful ways my inner wildness comes alive is in nature's embrace. Here, creativity feels effortless—spontaneous movements, words, and expressions emerge organically, unfiltered and free.

As I reflect on my life, searching for those untamed moments, I remember childhood afternoons rolling down a grassy hill in the neighborhood park with friends. We tumbled freely, laughing, our bodies expanding into space, the earth catching us with each descent.

Another memory surfaces, one of the most profound experiences of my life. In my twenties, I traveled to a remote town called Chaltén in Patagonia, near Fitz Roy. The winds were so fierce they could spin me around, and the endless sky, ablaze with stars, reflected off the ice of the glacier. I stayed for three months. At first, the relentless rain and intense weather unsettled me, but as the days passed, something shifted. It felt as if layers of conditioning years of learned responses and societal expectations were being stripped away, revealing something raw, and conditioned ways of responding to life.

One morning, I rose with the first light and waded into the lake freezing, naked, awake. The cold water jolted my bones, piercing through every layer of me. But as I emerged, I felt the rush of warmth flooding back my blood surging, my breath steadying, my clothes once again sheltering my body. It became my ritual. Each morning, I would submerge myself in the lake, then sit in stillness before the vast magnificence of the Andes wrapped in silence until the sun rose high enough to kiss my skin with its warmth.

Those months in Patagonia were a deep soul detox from the urban world. I became part of something wilder, something purer. I found joy in having nothing. Sitting at sunset, watching the pink clouds swirl and dance across the sky, or simply sharing a quiet gaze with another human—these were sacred moments. Just *being* was enough.

Is it possible to live like that all the time?

At that time, I didn't have the courage to even ask myself that question. I was young, adventurous, still trying to figure out life. But as I boarded the bus back to Buenos Aires, an ache settled in my chest. I couldn't stop crying, I felt like I was heading to prison.

The months that followed were hard. The city felt suffocating, a relentless jungle of concrete and noise. I struggled to find my place, to remember what it felt like to be *wild*. But there were moments, small acts of defiance, where I reconnected with that untamed state of being. Riding my bike at midnight, the streets empty, the wind on my face it carried whispers of Patagonia's fierce, untethered air. Dancing until I lost myself, my body surrendering to rhythm and sweat. Loving with the raw intensity of a body set free, unraveling in the ecstasy of release. In those moments, I touched freedom again.

Today, I recognize that art is another doorway to my wild self. My artistic languages weave together movement, words, music, and painting—a tapestry of expression that connects me to something deeper. As a child, painting and free play were moments when I felt most at home, slipping effortlessly into my natural state of being.

A few years ago, I faced a near-death experience, a health crisis that stripped me down to my essence. Perhaps it wasn't a wild memory in the traditional sense, but it brought me closer to the raw core of my existence. In the midst of this storm, a friend invited me to a workshop where we created a sacred space to express our emotions through art. I turned my room into a sanctuary, taping large sheets of white paper to my mirror and setting up a small altar—a table holding my acrylics, brushes, and the quiet intention to heal.

I was fighting to survive. But that blank canvas became an invitation—not just to create, but to *let go*. To give myself permission to *be*. I painted with no plan, no limits, leaving the process open for days. Shadows, colors, emotions—all merged on the page, a testimony of my journey. Not a story of illness, but of love. Of embracing my life, even in its uncertainty.

That act of creation became a ritual, a daily invitation to listen deeply, to meet myself with honesty. Each brushstroke opened a channel of intuition, a whisper of joy. It helped me shift my focus away from fear and pain, guiding me instead toward the small light within me. And as I painted, that light grew, expanding beyond the canvas—until I could feel it inside me once more.

© Marcela Sabin

As I reflect on this question, I return to the words of my teacher, a passage that resonates deeply:

> "Two of the most basic drives in humanity are the drive for safety and survival, and the drive to express, grow, explore, and create. The innate creature-level need for security, combined with the human longing for expression and the exploration of possibility, creates a dynamic tension in our lives—one that, at its best, is exhilarating and deeply fulfilling, and at its worst, can be painful, damaging, even emotionally, spiritually, and physically lethal." **–Michelle Masters**

I appreciate this quote from Michelle Masters because it invites us to explore the two fundamental forces that drive us as humans: the instinct for survival, which can sometimes consume us, and the deep longing to express, explore, grow, and create. Both are real, both are necessary—but without safety, creativity struggles to flourish. And without creativity and expression, our soul withers.

May this awareness help us find a balance—a way to transform while embracing both security and expansion. May it serve as an invitation to humanity to live with more joy and freedom.

When we step into that space of wildness, something shifts. Magic unfolds in many areas of our lives. The question of where we lost our connection to our wild self is, in truth, an invitation—a guide leading us back home to ourselves.

So, how do we return to this wild state of being while navigating the reality of safety and survival?

AN INVITATION TO ENTER

As a ceremonial practitioner, I have learned from my teachers that there is an intricate connection between the spiritual and material dimensions of life. Sometimes, we begin in the material world and work our way toward spirit; other times, we begin in the realm of spirit and bring its wisdom into our tangible reality.

I invite you to create a simple ritual—one that calls back your wildness.

How can you create a ritual to call back your wildness?

As we prepare for a ritual, we may choose an offering to give to the natural world flowers, tobacco, or something deeply meaningful to you or your lineage. Personally, I like to light a candle or create a small fire, bringing water or other sacred elements to form an altar. These are my ways of beginning, but I invite you to create your own ritual, one that aligns with your soul's knowing.

To begin, take a moment to connect with yourself. Become present to your breath. Notice the feeling of air moving through your nostrils, expanding into your lungs, then gently releasing as you exhale. This breath is life.

Now, bring your awareness to your heart. Feel its rhythm, its presence. Let your attention travel through your body, seeking that deep center where your connection to yourself resides.

Then, declare your intention to welcome wildness back into your life. Speak it aloud or hold it silently in your heart let it be true, clear, and deeply felt.

When you are ready, call upon your spirit. Let it know your intentions as you offer your gift to the earth, water, air, or fire.

Speak to spirit as you would to a dear friend or loved one. Open your heart. Allow yourself to be fully present in this exchange.

Now, visualize yourself in the state you long to embody. Feel the energy, the emotions, the aliveness that come with it. Let this vision settle into your being, expanding within you.

With this, the gate to your wild self begins to open.

JOURNALING AND REFLECTION:

Take the time to find a special notebook.

Choose one that speaks to your soul—decorate it, make it your own. I personally love white pages, spiraled to allow the flow of creativity without interruption. It becomes your sacred space for art and writing.

When you are ready, meditate on the questions below, allowing your heart to open, and then open your journal.

ASK YOURSELF WITH CURIOSITY:

- When was my life connected to my wildness?

Take a step back and recapitulate your life. This may take time, but the insights you'll gain are profound. Reflect on these questions:

- How did my wildness serve me in that moment?
- What qualities within myself did I recognize?
- How did it feel in my body?
- How was I in relation to others, and to the world around me?

Immerse yourself in these past experiences, as if you are living them again in the present moment. Track the gifts, the lessons, and the resources you find within them.

Allow yourself the freedom to journal, draw, and express—let whatever comes flow freely, with no judgment.

Identify a specific goal or result you want to achieve by reconnecting with your wildness.

For example, you might envision having more energy for creativity, a deeper connection to adventure, or an intuitive openness that feels aligned with your true self.

Describe this goal in vivid detail. How does it look? How does it feel? Imagine it fully:

- How do you picture it?

Is it vibrant in color, or more muted? Is it still, like a photograph, or dynamic, like a video?

- What sounds accompany it?
- What feelings arise within you as you connect with this vision—emotionally, energetically, or physically?
- What smells might be tied to this experience?
- What words would you use to capture the essence of having achieved this goal?

Creating change and incorporating it into your life is a process that requires patience and commitment. As Michelle Masters wisely says:

> *"The amount of time it takes to form a habit depends on the habit and the person. Building a habit of drinking a glass of water in the morning, for example, is generally easier than forming a daily habit of running five miles."* **Michelle Masters**

For me, change is rooted in motivation and desire. When I release the pressure of feeling like I "have to" change, and instead embrace the joy of reclaiming my true self, my motivations deepen.

Change becomes a loving commitment to myself—one that supports joy, awareness, and new possibilities in my life.

So, I make it my intention to embrace my natural child—my wild self—each day. I take moments to connect, listen, and choose an expression of my wildness, whether through movement, creativity, or simply being.

As I share these humble experiences with you, I invite you to embark on your own beautiful journey back to yourself.

BIOGRAPHY

Marcela Sabin, M.A., is a soul midwife, teacher, spiritual counselor, and coach who uses her diverse gifts to help people shift grief, trauma, anxiety, low self-esteem, and shame into transformative healing. She holds a degree in Psychology and Expressive Movement from Argentina and a Master's in Indigenous Mind. Marcela has spent years learning from traditional healers, Elders, and Wisdom Keepers across the globe, integrating these teachings with modern therapeutic practices to offer a unique perspective. She bridges these healing modalities, welcoming the whole person while offering spiritual support available to us all. Marcela has completed two years of Hakomi training—a mindfulness and somatic healing practice and is currently in training in Gestalt, both of which focus on the present moment and empower deeper access to consciousness as a pathway to healing.

WILD WOMAN PHOTOSHOOT

Abby Kojola

Written before my wild woman photoshoot:

- Who is my wild woman self?
- What does she long for?
- How does she move through the world?
- How does she move her body?
- How does the skin of her face rest and rejuvenate?
- How does it feel when pleasure rises through her, from the root of her being, and bursts throughout her entire body?
- How does she move when she no longer cares who is watching or what they think of her?

She walks through the world with confidence, her body sturdy, solid, and proud, swaying her hips in rhythm with the pleasure the friction creates between her legs. Any who would dare judge her indulgence in her own pleasure? Fuck them. Let them be left behind in her wake.

Her mouth is wide open, breathing in all the air she can, filling her deep, wide lungs, expanding her chest and lifting her breasts high, letting them bounce with every breath.

Her hair flows freely in the wind, brushing against her neck, breasts, and back in wild, silken waves. She tilts her head back and laughs as the wind shifts, tossing her hair across her face. With a smile, she runs her fingers through the thick strands, massaging her scalp, sending a shiver down her spine.

Her hips are wide, her belly soft, her curves unapologetically present. The breeze caresses her as her naked body moves forward, taking up all the space it needs, all the space it deserves.

Her feet are solid, sinking into the earth with every sacred step. They kiss the ground beneath her, embraced by the warm, soft soil, and the exchange of energy with the earth fills her with joy.

Her shoulders are strong, wide, and powerful. She releases tension, letting them relax down her back, while the skin of her back stretches and moves over the muscles beneath. She leans back, opening her heart to the sky, and reaches upward, drawing the warmth of the sun into her body. She is an extension of the earth, a creation of the universe—beautiful, curvy, and free.

Written after my wild woman photoshoot:

I embraced this project as my wild woman. She leaped at the opportunity, pouring everything into it—her creative energy surged. My wild woman has creativity pulsing through her veins.

I began with the inspiration of large, curvy bodies in print. What do I love seeing? Curves. Women loving their curves. Not hiding them. My wild woman hides nothing. She walks through the world owning every part of her, every cell of her being. She loves herself fiercely, from the inside out. She knows it is safe for her to be seen because her energetic boundaries are impenetrable. She's in control of who stays outside and who she invites in.

As a wild woman of the earth, I am in an intimate relationship with both the earth and my body. Time and again, I've laid my body on the earth, letting her cradle me completely. My trust in her is deep, endless. She holds all of me, absorbing my pain, my anguish, and infusing me with her strength, resilience, and groundedness until I become one with her. There is no difference between my body and the earth. I pray to remember this connection every moment I walk upon her; every time my sensitive feet and tender skin touch her surface. My feet kiss her, a sensual connection with the earth, with each sacred step, feeding and supporting me fully as I express myself.

The earth expresses herself in countless ways—those are me, too. The calm lakes, the furious oceans, the thunderstorms, the stunning sunsets, the fierce fires, and the warm, clear days that smile upon the universe. I am all of it. Every nuance, every extreme, is contained within my skin, and it is all allowed to exist—without shame, without judgment.

My wild woman controls when and how she expresses her wildness. She flows with the untamed energy of the earth. When she craves the serenity of the bay, met by the retreating tide, she enters anyway. The water calls her, beckoning her deeper. It whispers, "Sink into my soft, muddy embrace. Let me cover you with my love."

My wild woman literally infused herself with the smooth, rich mud beneath the Bay, as the tides moved in and out. It was exhilarating to sink my hands into the earth, spreading the mud all over my legs, thighs, ass, stomach, arms, and breasts. The sensation was so fucking sexy and sensual—being so intimately connected with this sacred, alive substance. Every movement felt like a declaration of presence, a visceral bond with the earth itself.

Candace was there, witnessing me through her lens, capturing these intimate moments. She gave me the gift of time, time to let my wild woman essence rise, time to claim this second and squeeze every ounce of desire and instinct into the experience.

Part of me doesn't even care what the images will look like, though I know they'll be wild and beautiful. What matters most is the feeling I had in that moment—the pleasure of indulging myself fully. The thrill of being immersed so deeply in the earth, surrounded by her gooey, soft, muddy glory.

I bought myself sunflowers and hugged them to my chest, loving the softness of the petals against my skin. I held a bunch of flowers in each hand, dragging their strong, bright yellow bursts through the water, throwing sprays of water into the air. Each splash created rainbows of muddy droplets that fell all over my body, shimmering in the sunset light.

My wild woman stood strong, sinking deeper into the mud, swaying in the warm glow of the setting sun. She sang to the sun, the earth, the water—celebrating all that binds us together. Candace placed tiny yellow flowers in my wild hair, a gesture of adornment that felt so natural. I love to decorate myself with flowers, earth, and everything that is born of nature.

I also loved the moments when Cami curled my hair, brushed my face with soft makeup brushes, and painted my lips bright red. I don't often take the time to do my hair or paint my face, but sometimes, it feels so fun and exciting. I love the attention. I am really good at receiving it. My wild woman welcomes attention with grace, effortless and unapologetic. It fuels her open heart, deepening her love, allowing her to love even more fully, without hesitation.

My wild woman receives beautifully. She receives herself in her fullness, embracing every desire that stirs within her. She welcomes every gift the abundant earth offers, allowing its richness to nourish her. She receives the pure love and attention of those who honor and respect her, basking in their reverence.

There are those who yearn to be received by her, to share in the raw, untamed experience of wildness the kind that blooms when control is gently set down, released like a whisper into the wind. In that space, pure possibility unfolds. Pleasure awakens. Joyful expression bursts forth, propelling life forward in an untamed, unfiltered dance.

We are always moving forward together, even when distance separates us. We are all wild at our core. We exist in the same mud of life, tangled in its raw, messy, unpredictable beauty. That mud can feel like a crisis, thick and unrelenting, clinging to everything we once wanted to keep pristine, controlled. Or—it can be exhilarating. A surrender. A moment to simply be stuck, immersed, and alive in the movement that thrums beneath the surface, pulsing in every breath, in every second.

My wild woman wonders, "How can I be most fully present in this moment of stuckness? Can I dig deeper into it? Can I sink my hands into the thick, wet earth, scoop it up, and smooth it over my body—let it seep into my skin until I embody it completely?"

This is how my wild woman meets her stuckness. It is both a defiant "Fuck You" and an intimate "Come Here." She does not push it away. She does not fear it. She whispers, "I love you. I will embrace you so fully that we dissolve into each other, transforming into something new, something alive, something moving, something free."

This is the medicine of stuckness, the alchemy I never understood until I allowed it to teach me.

That is the gift of my wild woman. She has the vision for connection, for breaking through perceived barriers, for finding new movement and freedom by dismantling her own walls. Yet, she carries her less wild parts with tenderness, never ignoring or dissociating from them. Instead, she holds them fully within her loving embrace, integrating all aspects of herself.

When it's just me, the earth, my wild woman, and the eyes of those who see me authentically—who desire nothing more than my total freedom, happiness, and truest expression—anything is possible. And when the setting isn't quite so supportive, generous, or ideal… anything is still possible. The eagle-eyed vision of my wild woman perceives a pathway through anything life delivers. She focuses with unwavering intensity, has no time for illusions, and dedicates herself to the boundless possibilities that arise from a deep connection with oneself, the earth, and others.

We all have a wild woman inside. Men, especially, have a wild woman inside. Find her. Surrender to her. Let her show you the way. Bow to her in gratitude. She comes from and is fueled by the earth, by the womb that gave you life. She wants you to claim your life, your whole, unfiltered, unrestrained life, with all its highs, lows, and every nuance that is uniquely yours. Do not miss any of it.

If you can receive her fully, you will notice there is no need to grasp, force, or struggle. Life moves at exactly the right pace, flowing in precisely the right ways. This is how your-our-life force works. Life itself is the force; we are merely its vessels. We open, soften, and allow it to exist, to move us forward. We honor it as sacred. In doing so, we honor ourselves and extend that reverence to others.

BIOGRAPHY

Abby Kojola lives in San Rafael, California, at the edge of China Camp State Park. A devoted student of the natural world, she finds wisdom in the whispers of plants, trees, birds, tides, water, land, elements, seasons, and stars. Her creative expressions include writing, mandala-making, cooking, baking, and nurturing deep friendships. She shares her home with beloved cats and deepens her understanding of life and self through prayer with plant medicines, both in community and solitude in nature.

A practice that brings Abby joy is composing Haiku poems inspired by her hikes. You can find these reflections on Instagram @haiku_hike. Since 2009, she has supported healers, creatives, and small business professionals through her expertise in website design, graphic design, and coaching. As the founder of Kojolapower WordPress Website Design, she blends creativity with strategy to help others share their gifts with the world. Discover her work at Kojolapower.com.

ALLOWING CREATIVE INSPIRATION FROM OUR NATURAL ENVIRONMENTS

Anin Utigaard

When I think of the term "inner wild," I am instantly transported back to my childhood wondrous moments spent exploring the untamed beauty of the forest during family camping trips or wandering through my backyard in Washington State, where my father nurtured a thriving apple tree heavy with red fruit. As a child, those natural spaces became the canvas for my imagination. My brother and I sculpted entire worlds in the dirt, transforming a hidden cove in the woods into a grand castle or an unshakable fortress. Each setting held limitless potential, shaped only by our boundless creativity and the roles we chose to inhabit.

Nature has always been a powerful force in my life, a wellspring of inspiration and renewal. When I immerse myself in nature, I feel a deep, unshakable connection to the Earth, a visceral awareness that I am part of something vast and sacred. It is in these moments that I also sense the presence of a higher power, an unseen spirit woven into the fabric of the natural world. Even as an adult, I carve out time in my demanding schedule to seek solace in the wilderness. Whether embracing the familiar comfort of a nearby wooded retreat or venturing onto a newly discovered trail, I know that each encounter with nature will leave me more grounded, more at peace, and infinitely more inspired.

NATURE AND EXPRESSIVE ARTS WITH CHILDREN

My graduate degree in Clinical Psychology included a specialty in Expressive Arts Therapy, led by our incredible teacher and program director at the time, Ben Hedges. One of the program's requirements was to design and implement a process for the Summer Camp sponsored by the university. The camp welcomed a diverse group of children, ranging from six years old to pre-teens, coming from varied background, some from wealthy families, others from single-mother households, private schools, and public schools, all with different cultural experiences.

Ben envisioned giving these children an opportunity to connect through expressive arts in nature while fostering relationships across different backgrounds.

At night, Ben would gather the young campers around the campfire, weaving stories that transported them to imaginary places and times. His storytelling was mesmerizing. He was not only a gifted narrator but also a bagpipe player and a clown, using his many talents to captivate and engage children.

I had also been trained by Natalie Rogers, daughter of Carl Rogers, who introduced the world to the Person-Centered method, also known as the Client-Centered approach. Natalie combined her father's philosophy with her mother's deep love for creativity, founding the Person-Centered Expressive Therapy Institute near Santa Rosa, California. After training with her, I began teaching alongside her, fully immersing myself in this transformative program. I knew this was the way I wanted to work with others, to empower them, to help them listen to their own needs, and to support their process of expression, release, engagement, imagination, and creation. I learned that when we provide a safe, non-judgmental space, whether for adults or children, we create opportunities for exploration, expression, insight, new awareness, and sometimes even healing.

For my contribution to the Expressive Arts Summer Camp, I drew inspiration from my own childhood. My brother and I used to craft imaginary worlds in the dirt near our grandmother's house. We built ranches with fences made from whatever materials we could find. Rocks became animals, horses, cows, pigs. while twigs carved out roads and marked the entrances to our miniature homes. Those experiences of boundless creativity and freedom informed the foundation of my approach.

I also applied my knowledge of the Child-Centered or Person-Centered approach. I believed that if I could create an experience that truly belonged to the children one in which they felt free to build whatever they desired, it could be profoundly empowering, fostering both emotional and cognitive growth.

Drawing from this, and inspired by Carl Jung's experience with creating miniature worlds, I introduced an activity to my assigned group on the first morning of camp. I asked each camper to find a special spot in the surrounding campground—a place that felt like it belonged to them during their time at camp. They were instructed to only use natural materials that were already loose rocks, branches, twigs, fallen leaves, nothing that required force to remove. If it resisted, it stayed where it was.

Their task? To create their own world. I provided examples: a castle, a farm, a vision of their future home, or a mysterious land hidden in the woods. But I also emphasized that there was no right or wrong way to do this. It was their world, entirely of their own making. My role was simply to grant them permission to create it.

For the next hour or two, they worked in focused, imaginative silence, lost in their personal landscapes. When they finished, we gathered as a group, and one by one, each child had the opportunity to guide us through their world. The excitement was beyond anything I had anticipated. They could hardly wait their turn, their enthusiasm bubbling over as they led us to their sacred spaces.

"This is my wishing well," one child beamed.

"And this is my lake," another announced proudly, their eyes shining.

Many created roads and animals; wishing wells appeared frequently. There were huts and castles, fences, and magical orchards brimming with abundance. Each creation was unique, a pure reflection of the child's imagination.

As we toured the spaces, the children's joy was contagious. They took immense pride in their work, reveling in their ability to shape and share something entirely their own. Many had intuitively built their worlds in circular formations—something I found fascinating, as I had never suggested it. Several asked if they could keep their creations intact for the duration of camp. When we agreed, they cheered, jumping up and down with excitement.

This experience taught me so much about the power of creativity. I saw firsthand how the activity shifted the children's moods, boosting their confidence and self-esteem. When parents visited, their children eagerly led them to their creations, proudly showcasing their work. I gently suggested that the parents avoid critiquing their child's piece—this was a deeply personal experience, and their pride in their artistic endeavor was something I didn't want diminished.

Even now, I wonder how many of those children carried this experience with them into adulthood. Did it spark a passion for design, architecture, or storytelling? Did it awaken something within them that continued to grow? No doubt, for them and for me, it was a memorable, transformative moment.

NATURE AND EXPRESSIVE ARTS FOR ADULTS

Several years later, after I had become a licensed Marriage and Family Therapist, I began offering expressive arts groups and retreats that combined creativity with exploration and connection to Mother Earth. My goal was to encourage new awareness and deeper relationships between participants and the natural world.

Before the devastating Northern California fires ravaged our tree-filled towns and wooded areas, a colleague and I hosted a three-day retreat at a center near Calistoga, California. The small ranch provided food and cabins, and a large hall where we gathered each morning and evening. The retreat's purpose was to inspire participants to reconnect with nature and discover what drew them to a particular animal, plant, or element of the landscape. I hoped they would begin to feel their connection to the world around them—realizing that we are all part of it.

Each morning, we formed a circle, set an intention for the day, and shared any dreams or reflections from our interactions with nature. We delved into discussions on ecopsychology and the profound value of connecting with the wild spaces around us.

Then, participants stepped outside into the natural world, allowing themselves to be drawn to a particular aspect of it. Was it a frog, a tree, a stream, a bird, or even the rustling sound of wind through the grass? Once something called to them, they were invited to sit with it—to observe without expectation, to notice both similarities and differences, and to simply be present.

I encouraged them to enter into a dialogue with their chosen plant, animal, or natural element. With a journal in hand, they asked a question and responded with their non-dominant hand, letting intuition guide the process. There was no judgment, only openness to whatever surfaced.

If they felt inspired, they could express their experience through a creative medium—perhaps a song, a movement, a poem, a story, or a piece of visual art. The focus was not on the final product, but on the deepened relationship with the natural world.

The morning was theirs to explore at their own pace. I wanted them to immerse themselves without feeling rushed, and if more time was needed, I allowed it. This was sacred time—an opportunity to forge a connection with nature, something we rarely give ourselves permission to do.

After lunch, we reconvened in the meeting hall. Participants were invited, but never obligated, to share their experiences. Poetry and journal entries were read, artwork adorned the walls, and one participant even created a rhythmic beat that the group followed while she moved and vocalized her connection to a farm goat she had bonded with. The goat had been particularly curious about our group, making the experience all the more meaningful.

For me, a willow tree became my muse. It offered me hours of inspiration—a song, a poem, a new way of seeing the world. Its flowing branches became a powerful symbol, reminding me to move with life's currents rather than resist them. I often reflect on that moment and the deep insight it provided.

Each person's offering enriched the group, creating a tapestry of shared experiences. The participants came from diverse backgrounds—some had traveled from as far as Japan—yet nature had woven us together in a profound and lasting way. Some bonded with trees, others with butterflies, bees, and birds. Some connected to the mountains, fields, or the quiet pond nearby. Each connection deepened our collective understanding of the intricate web of life that surrounds us, reminding us that we are never truly separate from the living world.

THE TAKEAWAY - FINDING OUR INNER WILD AND CONNECTING WITH NATURE

From these two experiences, I gained a profound appreciation for our role on this planet and a deeper understanding of the vital connection between humanity and the Earth. Now, more than ever, this connection is critical. If we continue to separate ourselves from nature, we risk sabotaging not only our own existence but also the survival of every living being that calls this planet home.

This union between humans and nature is not just beneficial—it is essential for our evolution. Nature, in its purest form, is our greatest teacher. A tree, with its twisting limbs, adapts to its surroundings, bending and stretching to find its place. A bird constructs its nest with intricate precision, weaving together shelter and security. The sky transforms into an ever-changing masterpiece, painting sunrises and sunsets in breathtaking hues.

When we allow ourselves to observe, meditate on, and absorb the magic of nature's creativity, something within us shifts. This experience isn't just beautiful—it's transformational. For children and adults alike, embracing the wonder of the natural world fosters a deeper sense of connection, inspiration, and belonging.

Use your imagination to craft an experience—one that invites others to connect deeply with the Earth. It sounds simple, yet too often, we deny ourselves the time and freedom to truly immerse in nature's embrace.

As expressive arts therapists, we have the power to create intentional spaces where others can step away from daily distractions and engage in profound, transformative experiences with Mother Earth. Through these moments of connection, we help dissolve the barriers of detachment, allowing a renewed sense of unity between nature and ourselves to take root.

BIOGRAPHY

Anin Utigaard is a Licensed Marriage and Family Therapist and a Registered Expressive Arts Therapist. She works with individuals and groups across diverse ages and cultures, integrating creativity and therapeutic practice to foster healing and transformation.

As a founding member of the International Expressive Arts Therapy Association (IEATA), Anin served as an Executive Core Committee (ECC) member and continues to contribute as part of the Advisory Council. She was a faculty member at Natalie Rogers' Person-Centered Expressive Therapy Institute for over a decade, where she deepened her commitment to the person-centered approach in both client work and teaching.

Anin currently serves as adjunct faculty at the Northwest Creative and Expressive Arts Institute in Seattle, Washington, and previously held an adjunct faculty position at JFK University until her relocation in 2017. Since 1992, she has shared her expertise through national and international workshops, presentations, and training programs.

With a background in fine arts and professional music, Anin blends artistic expression with psychology and a humanistic approach to psychotherapy. She firmly believes in the transformative power of the arts to heal individuals and create positive change in the world.

© Nicki Koethner

EXPANDING ATTACHMENT THEORY: THE ARMS OF INFINITY AND BEYOND

Martha Hines

How often do you wish someone would say, "It's all okay"? How often do you long for someone to look you in the eyes and say, "You are perfect and completely, infinitely loved just the way you are"? How often do you wish that your mother, your father, a grandparent, or a caregiver were around to do that, no matter how old you are? And what if the answer to all of these longings was much closer than we realize? Do you ever sit under a tree, listen to the wind, and feel the breeze moving over your skin?

Have you sat by the ocean, drifting on the sound of the waves as they move in and out? Have you allowed yourself to wander up through the night sky, sitting with the moon, or even beyond, into the solar system, the Milky Way, or the infinity of the All That Is? Have you ever laid in bed at night, feeling sick or distraught, and sensed the arms of the divine or the light of God surrounding you? Filling you? Offering a sense that you are not alone?

Have you ever felt yourself shift into an overwhelming sense of joy, gratitude, or deep, infinite love just from a single "touch" of divine light?

Twenty years ago, like many of us, I studied attachment theory in college and graduate school. I became a clinical social worker and psychotherapist specializing in trauma and attachment work.

I learned about the infamous Bowlby monkey experiment, which demonstrated—albeit with questionable ethics—that touch and attachment are fundamental to life and well-being. This research revealed that the attachment style we develop as children follows us throughout life, significantly influencing our ability to lead happy, emotionally healthy lives.

As a social worker and psychotherapist, I spent many years helping parents care for highly traumatized children. My primary focus was guiding these caregivers in salvaging, as much as possible, the attachment development of children who had suffered severe abuse and neglect.

This work was challenging, but the good news was that many of these children had caregivers willing and capable of consistently providing them with love and care. In contrast, working with adults to help them cultivate a stronger sense of emotional grounding, centeredness, and well-being proved far more difficult. As adults, we typically lack the parental figures who once provided care for us as children.

Many—perhaps most—of us long for a constant, caring, and unconditionally loving parental figure to hold us, nurture us, and reassure us that we are safe, valued, and cared for. Some of us experienced this in childhood, while others did not. Most of us had parents who, like us, were imperfect, making our childhoods a mixture of positive and negative attachment experiences. But as we grow older, we realize that even if we once had that unconditional care, the experience is now a distant memory.

Psychotherapists attempt to address this void in various ways—through the unconditional positive regard offered in the therapeutic relationship, through techniques such as Dialectical Behavioral Therapy, and through other approaches aimed at fostering emotional resilience. These methods are often effective and undoubtedly have their place. However, I propose another, expanded perspective on attachment theory that has implications for how we heal our attachment wounds.

Over the past few years, the spirit world has been nudging me to recognize the revolutionary potential of expanding our understanding of "attachment figures" and the essence of an ultimate caregiving presence in our lives.

Here is what the spirit world has been reminding me:

Even as grown adults, even if our parents have passed on, even if we never had parents or consistent, loving caregivers—regardless of our circumstances—we are always cradled in the infinite embrace of the Earth, the cosmos, existence itself, and the divine.

We often hear the phrase, "the arms of the divine." But have we truly expanded our concept of attachment to include not just human figures, but the Earth itself, the cosmos, and all of existence? What shifts within us when we embrace this broader perspective? How does it transform our sense of belonging and support?

What if our attachment figures are not solely human—traditionally a mother or father—but extend beyond the physical realm? What if our concept of "attachment" encompasses the Earth, the cosmos, existence itself, and the divine?

The truth is, we are not separate from these forces. We are beings of the Earth, woven from the fabric of the cosmos, part of the infinite dance of existence and divinity. Just as we were once sheltered within the womb of our mothers, we are eternally held in the vast and nurturing "womb" of the Earth, the cosmos, existence itself, and the divine.

One could argue that the traditional model of attachment development taught in psychology classes and graduate programs is limited, even from a cultural standpoint. I was taught that we form a singular, or perhaps two, primary attachment figures. This might hold true for some upper-middle-class, Caucasian households in Western societies today. But what happens when we shift our perspective?

Imagine placing the notion of an "attachment figure" into a joint family household or a village culture, where a child is raised by multiple, equally present caregivers. How does this reframe our understanding of attachment formation? Or consider children who enter full-time daycare at three months old, how does this change our sense of attachment formation?

Beyond human relationships, what if we expand our definition of attachment to include the Earth itself? Just as caregivers rock us as infants, we are perpetually cradled by the Earth's rhythmic movements—its rotation on its axis, its orbit around the sun. Our relationship with the cosmos is no different. We are engaged in an endless, silent dance with the moon. The tides remind us of this pull, an ebb and flow that extends beyond metaphor, shaping even our physical world.

When we lie beneath a vast sky, staring into the luminous stretch of the Milky Way, awe and wonder naturally arise. Looking "up into the stars," we glimpse only a fraction of an infinite cosmic expanse—one that holds not just our planet but us, individually and collectively. What if we allowed ourselves to feel that holding?

Our need to be held is real. It does not disappear with age, nor is it without purpose. And, astonishingly, even in moments of isolation, we are always held—by the Earth, by the cosmos, by existence itself.

What if, rather than longing solely for a mother, father, or caregiver—whether present or absent—we could acknowledge that longing while simultaneously surrendering into the embrace of the Earth, the very substance from which we are formed?

What if we could relax into the knowing that we are cradled, always, by the infinite expanse of the universe? And for those who believe in a divine presence, what if we could trust that we are continually held in the unending arms of the divine?

- *How does this feel in our bodies?*
- *How does this feel in our souls?*
- *How does this feel for our hearts?*

How does this feel for our weary, tired, scared, worried, angry, sorrowful, grieving, sometimes hopeless, sometimes elated, sometimes overjoyed, sometimes transcendent, and sometimes simply confused selves—those of us doing our very best to navigate this life on the planet we call Earth?

I think we need all the help we can get. And perhaps, we are overlooking a profound source of support—one that has always been there, waiting for us to remember its existence.

I offer this as a question, as a prayer, as an invitation for exploration, reflection, and conversation. This is a possibility—an opportunity—to reconnect with a reality that may help us feel more held, more seen, more centered, calm, and cared for. Even in our loneliest moments, we are never truly alone. There is something, someone, always present to lean on.

I would love to hear your thoughts, reflections, wisdom, and feelings on any of this. I send this to you with love, with an embrace—from one being of Earth, the cosmos, existence, and the divine, to another.

And so, it is. Amen.

BIOGRAPHY

Martha Alter Hines, MSW, is a mother, author, healer, and astrologer. With twenty years of experience as a clinical social worker, psychotherapist, and bodyworker, she brings a unique blend of trauma-informed care and astrological insight to her work. Her studies in Evolutionary Astrology with Ari Moshe Wolfe and Heather Ensworth have deepened her understanding of the intricate connections between the cosmos, Earth, and human experience.

Born in Thailand and raised in Bangladesh, Pakistan, Kenya, and the United States, Martha has cultivated a profound passion for alleviating suffering worldwide. She is dedicated to guiding others toward healing, wholeness, and the infinite wisdom that resides within us all Through her work, Martha seeks to help others thrive, reconnect with their innate healing abilities, and embrace the vast, interconnected beauty of existence. Email: <u>livingtheonelight@gmail.com</u>

Website: https://livingtheonelight.com

Facebook: https://www.facebook.com/livingtheonelight

YouTube: https://www.youtube.com/channel/UCgNGs08tGaA3AdK0LpuWJTg

Teachable Site: https://living-the-one-light.teachable.com

© Nicki Koethner

EARTH, THE SOUL, AND THE CREATIVE IMPULSE: A LIFE LED ON PURPOSE

Jo Burrows

Living fully and creatively, for me, is an exquisite balance between discipline, the kind that teaches us to pay attention and come into presence as a spiritual practice, and the art of letting go. It is in this delicate space that joy, revelation, and play emerge. A daring willingness to be present and engaged with the very elements of life are nature, our work, our relationships, even in the hard places. It is about embracing the moments of life, both beautiful and difficult, tossing them into the air, and saying, "Oh, let's take a look!" Not striving for perfection or having everything sorted out, but choosing to be authentically alive, with eyes wide open.

What I have learned most on this journey—a journey that has deepened, meandered, and rarely followed a straight path—is that creativity is a layered process, not necessarily a linear one. We begin with a foundation, much like constructing the hull of a boat. We acquire greater self-knowledge, refine our ways of thinking, and release what no longer serves us. Over time, with self-acceptance and compassion, something within us softens. We become more patient, more attuned to our bodies and our bones. And with guidance, we learn to trust our intuition and creative impulses. Only then can we allow the wind and the waves to be our guides.

Yet, sometimes, the process unfolds in reverse. We first feel the wind and the sea stirring within us, and only then does the desire arise to deepen our knowledge and awareness of the whole. But how do we sustain this creative drive and keep it alive? And more importantly, what is creativity, anyway?

What Is Creativity?

One of the more promising developments in recent decades has been our evolving understanding of creativity. We now embrace cross-specialization, intersectionality, neurodivergence, and a greater tolerance for complexity and dissonance. We recognize that creativity is not confined to a single domain—it is fluid, multifaceted, and deeply intertwined with both logic and intuition.

When I was growing up in the 70s and 80s, the prevailing mindset was different. You were either artistic and creative or technical and academic—especially in education, but also in the broader culture. The two were seen as distinct, rarely intersecting.

Following in my parents' footsteps, I took an academic path, never considering creativity as a viable pursuit, let alone something I could explore alongside my studies. This rigid division led to a kind of impoverishment—like being allowed only one type of nourishment, limiting the richness of experience and self-expression. It felt as if the natural process of wonder and curiosity was forced into a binary choice: this or that, one path or the other.

The kind of creativity I want to explore here is not solely about the long, disciplined journey of becoming a professional dancer, musician, or artist. Rather, it is about how we engage with all parts of ourselves—how we expand into the full spectrum of who we are meant to be. It is about realizing that our creativity is not an isolated phenomenon but a reflection of something greater, an intrinsic part of the creative universe we inhabit.

For those of us on a healing or spiritual path, this realization is not a one-time event but an ongoing process. It resurfaces again and again, often during transitions, challenges, or wake-up calls on our journey.

Waking up to a larger version of myself

"You can't approach your feelings as if it were a Ph.D."

My first invitation to awaken into a larger version of myself came at age 27 when I left an MA/Ph.D. program in moral philosophy. While deeply committed to learning, I had neglected my inner life, and my body rebelled—demanding attention in ways I could no longer ignore. Illness forced me to step away. But as the mythology of Saturn Return suggests, sometimes things must crumble before we recognize the path we are truly being called to walk. That path, for me, revealed itself through the therapeutic creative arts.

I was still in my university town in England when I encountered a creative therapeutic modality called psychodrama. Through role play, improvisation, and creative acting techniques, participants were encouraged to theatrically reenact old narratives and then craft new ones to live into. It was less about intellectualizing and more about surrendering to a kind of divine play.

Within this same space, I was introduced to authentic movement. On Sunday mornings, in a retreat-like setting, we would wake gently, share a homemade granola breakfast, and dance—allowing our bodies to move freely, trusting in the rhythm of the music and the warmth of the sun streaming through the windows. It was a practice of learning to let go.

One of the group leaders once said to me, "Jo, you can't approach your feelings like a Ph.D." Something shifted in that moment. We were being invited to connect with our emotions through our bodies—to release the tightly held scripts we had fought so hard to maintain. The group also incorporated Gestalt work, which emphasized the power of the present moment. Rather than simply dissecting our past, we explored how it emerged in the now.

Another leader asked, "Which bowl are you going to choose—the one filled with thumbtacks or the one overflowing with cherries?" The question lingered. It was a reminder that we have a choice in how we engage with life.

Years later, after completing a graduate program in psychology specializing in drama therapy, I felt privileged to bring this same transformative magic to others—both in group settings and individual practice. I had come to understand that self-knowledge is a balance between intellectual insight and creative embodiment, between mind and soul. True healing unfolds when we peel away the layers of outdated narratives and step into the truth of who we are.

Deepening my Buddhist meditation practice, I took my refuge vows, fully committing to the path. I remembered my first introduction to meditation in college—how profoundly it had shifted my understanding of self and existence. It had taught me three things:

a) At a cellular level, we are interconnected with the world around us.
b) Our intrinsic goodness is not something to earn—it is our natural state because we are not separate from existence itself.
c) We are not our thoughts.

Yet, despite these realizations, it is all too easy to forget.

Over time, my meditation practice expanded beyond the cushion—it became a way of living, a daily act of paying attention. I began teaching this to my clients, guiding them to truly see the world around them. What does it mean to fall in love with the world? To notice, to soften, to play, to let go? And where can nature hold not just our joy, but also our grief and pain?

For years, I led mindfulness walks in an outpatient hospital program for clients with moderate to severe mood disorders such as depression and anxiety. Together, we walked, not just moving through space but engaging with it. I invited them to experience the world differently, to embrace mindfulness in three simple yet profound steps:

- **Observe.** Look deeply. Immerse yourself in your surroundings—the vibrant blue of a jay's feathers, the weathered elegance of a Spanish door handle, the sturdy presence of a knobby oak tree. Engage all five senses. Let your thoughts drift in and out, acknowledging them as passing phenomena, and gently return your attention to the present moment.
- **Describe.** Articulate what you see as though you're capturing it in memory, the way people once did before cameras were ever-present. Imagine needing to paint the moment in your mind, pixel by pixel, so you can recall its richness later.
- **Connect.** This is the heart of it all—building a relationship with your surroundings. Allow yourself to be moved. Stretch out your hand in gratitude. Feel the unspoken dialogue between you and the world. Ask for guidance, not in words, but in presence. In these moments, we rediscover our deep, undeniable interconnection with nature.

After we returned from our walks, I would ask the clients to share their experiences—whether through words, writing, or drawing—about something that had touched or moved them. What captivated me most was witnessing how this immersion kept their moods uplifted for longer. It made me wonder: how else could I enrich this process?

One approach was guiding them to deepen their awareness of positive emotions as they arose. If they felt joy, I encouraged them to sit with it, to explore its texture. What did joy feel like? Where in the body did it emerge? Did it shimmer like sunlight on water, or did it hum like a quiet, steady pulse? What if there were thirty different shades of joy waiting to be named, experienced, and understood?

Inspired by the emerging work in Positive Psychology, I discovered researcher Barbara Fredrickson's list of ten positive emotions. I invited my clients to engage with them—joy, gratitude, serenity, interest, hope, pride, amusement, inspiration, awe, and love. Each of these emotions, universal and scientifically observed in brain scans, became a playground for exploration.

Somehow, knowing there was a scientific basis behind it made it more compelling to clients. Psychology has long focused on pathology, examining a vast spectrum of negative states. Yet, for years, little research had explored the science of happiness. No one had truly *asked*: What defines happiness? What are its core qualities?

Meanwhile, neuroscience was uncovering why our brains, almost by default, lean toward negativity—especially when it comes to long-term memory. Rick Hanson, a neuroscientist and psychologist, suggests this negativity bias may have an evolutionary edge. When something bad or dangerous happens, the brain stores it in long-term memory as a survival mechanism—to learn and avoid repeating the mistake. In contrast, positive experiences, unless extraordinary, tend to fade. They lack the same urgency for survival, slipping through the cracks of memory like water through open fingers.

Good Feelings as a Resource

But if this is true, how do we offset it? How do we tip the balance in our favor? More importantly, how do we learn to fully sink into our good feelings as a resource rather than letting them slip away?

Psychologist Rick Hanson suggests that to counteract the brain's natural negativity bias, we must make it a daily practice to absorb positive experiences intentionally. It takes just 60 seconds of focused attention to embed a moment into long-term memory—transforming a fleeting feeling into something lasting. Clients often find this approach both practical and achievable. One can either anchor into a positive experience that just occurred or deliberately seek one, a practice I often describe as depositing "positive chips" into the bank.

In my private practice, to enhance the experience, I invite clients to use the technique called tapping, commonly used in Eye Movement Desensitization and Reprocessing (EMDR)—a modality designed for trauma healing. While EMDR is primarily used to release trauma, it can also help solidify positive moments. As clients immerse themselves in a good experience, I might guide them to gently tap on their arms or legs, reinforcing the moment energetically and embedding it into long-term memory. Similarly, tapping can be used to reconnect with a past positive experience, serving as a powerful tool for re-remembering and resourcing.

Like with any technique I teach, I first try it on myself. Over time, I began referring to my downloads as "Postcard Moments." A squirrel darting across my path in the morning. A single dewdrop resting in perfect formation on a succulent. The subtle tilt of a stranger's smile.

Or while commuting—marveling at how the morning light drapes itself across the San Francisco Bridge like an artist's brushstroke, the crossbars forming perfect angles against the sky. Watching seagulls glide in seamless formation, as if orchestrating a silent message of love. Ordinary moments, yet they now feel like thousands of friendly beings populating my mind.

We all know that magic—that mystery, that wonder—when we truly capture a moment. When we inhale the breath of an ancient forest, feel the rhythm of the ocean, sense the pulse of the early morning breeze. When we trace the lines of a lover's hands as if deciphering a sacred script. In those instances, time doesn't just slow—it bends. Moments expand, stretching into something timeless. Long-distance runners know this. Swimmers feel it.

For me, swimming is not about exertion. It's not about 'exercise.' It's about becoming part of the water. Moving because the water asks me to. Because I am in direct play with the universe around me.

Many of us have wondered why, despite our ability to shift perspectives and be moved by the world around us, we don't do so more often. What holds us back from engaging fully, from stepping into a state of awe and flow at will? How do we go beyond simply practicing mindfulness and instead make it an intrinsic way of being—like slipping on a different pair of glasses and seeing the world anew?

In my experience, recognizing that we control the lens through which we view reality is an act of conscious choice. We are not separate from the world, though our thoughts often insist that we are. If the mind shapes our reality, how can we use it as an ally rather than an adversary? How do we allow ourselves to feel deeply touched by the world rather than numbed by it?

There's something inherently developmental in this process. We must first make peace with what is—our narratives, our emotions, our history—before we can fully embrace a new way of seeing. Otherwise, any attempt to cultivate positivity risks becoming an act of suppression rather than transformation.

Tilting toward the positive does not mean rejecting pain. Life's chaos, its darkness, and our own emotional turbulence are not to be denied. Every feeling—joy, grief, anger, wonder—serves a purpose. Sometimes, the most powerful thing we can do is simply sit with them.

Yet, as many spiritual traditions teach, if we learn to remain present with an emotion while bracketing the thought patterns that fuel suffering—seeing our thoughts as objects rather than absolute truths—we create space to endure and ultimately transcend our struggles. The pain itself does not break us. It is the stories we attach to it that hold the power to make us suffer.

Shifting away from old narratives is hard because they shape who we believe we are. But through meditative awareness and the cognitive discipline of tracking—not judging—our thoughts and emotions, we cultivate resilience. With self-compassion and a touch of playful humor, we learn not to take our inner stories so seriously.

In that awareness, a choice emerges. We can switch into a state of joyful engagement with ourselves, others, and the world—the realm of myth, poetry, dance, and mystical union. The unknown becomes a space of possibility, reminding us that we are not bound by old narratives. Learning to create intentions for what we want in our future, I believe also means creating a new language of sorts. Going from wanting to having, as we learn to trust the benevolence around us, and in the present tense declare: *I am opening to love; I am becoming more and more ready; I am imagining this future for myself because I see it already happening. For me, that is the ultimate act of creation.*

BIOGRAPHY

Jo Burrows is a psychotherapist, coach and mindfulness teacher with over 24 years' experience. As a longstanding Buddhist, and spiritual practitioner, Jo offers a warm and present centered approach that brings together her somatic and heart-based understanding of how we come to change as human beings. Trained in EMDR, Mindfulness based cognitive behavioral therapy, and the creative arts therapies for 16 years, Jo brings a creative and dynamic approach to her work. With extensive training also in coaching programs, Jo helps clients unearth unhelpful beliefs and patterns towards a more powerful way of living and being in joy. Her company, Compassionate Brain Life Coaching (CBLC) offers Transformational Coaching; Resiliency and Empowerment work; and business leadership mentoring that helps clients create purposeful and meaningful lives by design. Jo has a practice in Berkeley, CA, works for Google on their mental health team, and offers sessions for individuals, couples and groups.

ECOUTEARTH

Karina Colliat

My main form of art has been claying figure sculpture. I like getting my hands in the mud, moving it around, building, and tearing down, until a figure is formed. I am not afraid of going into the mess and trusting the process. Adding and taking away, there are no mistakes. It is a process of shaping, creating and destroying. The clay is amorphous, squishing between my fingers, separating and connecting, solid and yielding, moving. The clay holds energy from the earth and can easily bear the intense emotions that I channel into my creations.

I knew, deep in my bones, the healing power of Mother Nature when I worked as a wilderness therapy instructor with adolescents in the high desert of Idaho. For two weeks at a time, I lived under the open sky, my body syncing with the rhythms of the land. My senses sharpened. The scent of sagebrush and earth became richer, more distinct. My imagination stirred, vivid and untamed. My sight sharpened, my body grew stronger, and something within me—something ancient and knowing—reawakened.

When people asked about the wilderness therapy program, about what truly worked, I thought the healing was in the desert.

I was led to this work after experiencing the collective trauma of 911. I was ten blocks away from the Twin Towers when they fell. Witnessing this catastrophe sent me into shock. I wasn't able to feel much of anything. My body held onto fear and rage, pressing it deep inside. My mind, for the first time, confronted the raw reality of death and mortality. The fragility of life became undeniable. And in that stark awakening, a desire ignited within me—to live fully, to embrace each moment as if it were my last.

Through various journeys, that desire eventually led me to Idaho, where I worked with adolescents in the desert. In them, I saw reflections of my own struggles—people grappling with fear, loss, and the longing for something more. I realized I could help them understand themselves better, learn to communicate, and cultivate confidence. In doing so, they could find a greater sense of freedom in their lives. But I wasn't healing them alone. The desert itself was working its own magic.

Nature is bigger than all of us. It can hold our frustrations, pain, sadness, fear, and anger—just as it holds our joy and excitement. It does not judge. It simply absorbs, transforms, and continues. Nature teaches us the cycles of life and death, the intricate balance of all things. It reminds us that we are connected—to each other and to something far greater than ourselves.

In the wilderness, I discovered a new form of spirituality—one rooted in the land itself. I talk and listen to the rocks and trees. I hear wisdom in the songs of birds and the rustling of grasshoppers. I have a whole clan of spirit guides I call upon when I need strength, support, and clarity. I send my questions into the vast vessel of nature and listen for its quiet, unshakable truths.

My time in the desert made one thing clear: I want to help people heal through creativity and nature.

Many years later, I conceived the idea of a slow-down movement. On the night of the equinox, March 21, 2011, the wind beckoned to me. It whispered and roared, urging me to pause, to listen. The wind spoke with an undeniable force. I slowed down, stripped away distractions, and laid my bare body on the ground, feeling the Earth against my skin. I surrendered to the moment, breathing in the stillness, the raw connection. When I finally rose, I thanked the earth around me. As if in response, the wind gusted up, a brief, powerful acknowledgment.

That night, I was reminded of the profound importance of listening to the Earth. It had been only weeks since the devastating earthquake in Japan, and fear loomed over California. Rumors of "the big one" swirled. I had been watching my cat, knowing that animals sense the Earth's shifts long before we do. They leave, they act differently. It made me wonder if I tuned in deeply, if I truly listened, could I, too, sense what was coming? But it wasn't just about predicting earthquakes. It was about something deeper—reclaiming a right relationship with the land. I realized that just as balance and harmony in human relationships come through mutual listening and respect, so too does our relationship with nature. In that moment, I made a commitment—to slow down, to listen, to be present with the Earth.

Écouter means "to listen" in French. I take this word to heart. I spend time in nature, learning to listen in different ways. Sometimes, I sit in stillness, noticing the world with all my senses. I listen through my eyes when I paint, through my body when I move, through my words as I describe scents, sounds, and textures. Each moment reveals a new way to listen, a new way to understand. And so, I invite others to join me—to slow down, to listen, to be with the Earth, in the Earth, as part of the Earth.

Ecoutearth is a combination of mindfulness, ecopsychology, and expressive arts

Mindfulness is the practice of bringing our awareness fully into the present moment. This can take many forms, but a common technique is to focus on the breath—gently returning our attention to it whenever our thoughts begin to drift.

When we integrate ecopsychology into mindfulness, awareness expands beyond the breath. Ecopsychology explores the deep relationship between humans and the more-than-human world. We do not simply exist in nature; we are in constant relationship with it. Mindfulness in this context means noticing more—the feel of air against our skin, the temperature shifting around us, the subtle interplay of sound and silence, the dance of light and shadow, the textures beneath our fingertips.

What happens within you when you hear a bird's song? How does your body respond when fog rolls in, softening the edges of the world? These are not just observations; they reveal the intimate way we relate to our surroundings. Ecopsychology teaches us that our psychological well-being is deeply interwoven with the living, breathing world around us.

When we add expressive arts, it introduces a new way of relating—what is called an aesthetic response. But what does that mean? According to Paolo Knill, an aesthetic response "describes characteristic ways of being in the presence of a creative act or a work of art—ways that touch soul, evoke imagination, engage emotions and thought" (Minstrels of the Soul, p. 70). It is a way of forming a relationship with art, a conversation between you and the creative act itself.

For example, consider drawing a tree you see. Instead of merely glancing at it, you spend time truly seeing it—studying its contours, textures, and energy. Through the act of drawing, you become present with the tree in a way that deepens your perception. Or perhaps you explore movement in relation to the tree—standing tall, stretching, feeling what it's like to extend both into the earth and into the sky. Maybe you move like the wind dancing through its branches.

Music, too, becomes a form of connection. Like birds singing their songs, we can use our voices or instruments to send vibrations into the world—to animals, plants, the air itself. Or perhaps the landscape inspires words within you, poetic expressions longing to be spoken, sung, or written.

The core practice is listening. Listen with your heart, your ears, your eyes. Listen with your feet against the ground, with the rhythm of your breath, with the openness of your being. The Earth is always speaking—what does it say to you?

You, too, can practice Ecoutearth. It is as simple as calling yourself into presence with your surroundings. The practice deepens when done in nature. Take time to listen, and notice how you respond. If you're tired, lay on the ground and feel its support, offering gratitude as you do. You may dance, sing, hum, or simply walk in awareness—acknowledging the trees, rocks, streams, and the life around you. Say thank you. That's all there is to it. Now, go do it!

REFERENCES

Paolo J. Knill, Helen Nienhaus Barba, Margo N. Fuchs. (2004) Minstrels of Soul Intermodal Expressive Therapy

BIOGRAPHY

Karina Colliat has a Masters in Psychology with an emphasis in Expressive Art Therapy from the California Institute of Integral Studies (CIIS). She also uses Eco-psychology, Somatics therapy, and touch work. She is an artist. She draws, paints, and makes clay figure sculptures. In her 20's she studied and practiced Tibetan Buddhism. And throughout the years came to know Vipassana and Zen. While in Idaho she really came to appreciate nature. She felt at one with nature. It was her beginning of a shamanistic way of seeing the world. She spent many years practicing qi gong, and has delved into the world of expanded states of consciousness. She experienced a stroke in December 2022 which led her to about 9 months of bliss where everything was perfect. Now she is starting to work more spiritually, guiding people into the world she knows is possible. https://ecoutearth.weebly.com/

© Nicki Koethner

INTO THE WILD: THE DANCE OF EGO AND SOUL

Nicki Koethner

The wild creativity in me declares:

"Don't label and categorize me, my ingredients will elude you."

My wildness is not predictable; it is spontaneous and free. It grows as it must and withers with the seasons. It moves to an inner rhythm, pulsing with life, following the heart wherever it leads. It has no constructs, no agendas, no rigid plans—only an instinctual pull to roam with the winds, swim in the oceans, fly in the skies, and crawl upon the earth.

It is the flower breaking through cement, asserting itself despite the weight and density of the civilized world. It runs like wild horses across prairies and meadows, galloping along the shore, mane flowing with the wind.

It exists everywhere and nowhere, untethered by time and space. My hair is uncombed, my clothes crumpled and worn, punctuated with holes that tell their own stories.

I am kind yet undefined. My existence is shaped by presence, by breath, by the raw essence of being alive. Formed by all the elements, I cannot be captured—yet I endure within structures and thrive in chaos. PowerPoints, charts, and scales hold no interest for me. Wildness whispers, "Don't put me in a box or assign me a number. You'll only get lost trying."

The wild is an invitation—a call to move with the currents, to follow the impulses that lead me through the meadows of dreams and visions. It reinvents itself, shaping me into the crystallized essence of who I am.

Comparison does not exist within me. I burst into deep laughter for no reason at all, feeling the cosmic dance of it all. I also dwell in deep sobs, thunderstorms, and tempests. Volcanoes, hurricanes, and tornadoes may not make me seem appealing, but they are as much a part of my nature as the gentle breeze.

The wild in me resists structure and routine. The status quo is dull. I long for freedom—to do what brings me joy, to feel the wind on my skin, to watch children move unrestrained, their thoughts unhindered by limitations. I reject cages, prisons, and boxes, whether of brick and mortar or thought and form. I am most myself when I am free, when I love without constraint, when I watch leaves twirl in a dance with the wind.

My ego, however, struggles with my wildness. It craves direction, a map to guide its way. The wild does not mind the ego but will not be tamed by it. The ego desires recognition, validation. It bristles under criticism, frets over accomplishments. The wild, in contrast, simply is—unconcerned with opinions or expectations. The ego lives in the doing; the wild thrives in being. It is untamed, unpredictable, and unbothered by the narratives of 'not enough' or 'too much.'

The ego follows a timeline, bound by constructs, while the wild moves freely—untethered by concepts of gender, age, race, or ethnicity. The wild is not concerned with time but flows with the organic rhythm of existence, tapped into the soul and the intricate web of interconnectedness. It is part of the cosmic dance, existing beyond the confines of time and space.

The wild accomplishes simply by being itself—unconcerned with recognition yet deeply present. It touches life through its very essence, rippling with laughter and tears. It tells stories, sings songs, and dances without questioning its own meaning. It delights in the unexpected, rejoicing at the sight of a house that dares to break the mold of uniformity.

While the ego clings to complaints, resentments, and fears, the wild has already moved forward—embracing the next adventure. The ego seeks simplicity yet complicates everything with its need for control. The wild, in contrast, exists within paradox—holding both complexity and simplicity, stretching across seasons, oceans, and dimensions, immersed in the unknowable mystery of timelessness.

The wild is my multidimensionality—past, present, and future interwoven. It perceives templates, blueprints, and archetypal patterns beyond the personal, alchemizing the essence of my true self. It listens to its own rhythm, beyond expectation, beyond constraint, simply unfolding as it was always meant to be.

BIOGRAPHY

Nicki Koethner, MA, MFT, is a Somatic Expressive Arts Psychotherapist, Educator, Consultant, and Multi-media Artist specializing in transforming trauma into empowerment. Devoted to playfulness, joy, and embodied earth-based spirituality, she maintains a private practice in Berkeley, CA, and online in both English and German. She serves as adjunct faculty at Sofia University and the California Institute of Integral Studies (CIIS). She has also been an ECC and board advisor to the International Expressive Arts Therapy Association and former co-supervisor of an Expressive Arts Therapy Program at Contra Costa Health Services, where she provided training and supervision to MFT associates. She is a contributing author to "Anxiety Warrior Vol 2," "Anxiety meets Compassion" and contributing author to the Mental Health Trainer's Guide by Pacific Center for Human Growth: "Unlocking Stigma" working with LGBTQI2-S children, TAY, adults and older adults. Compassion Fatigue, Well-Being, And Burnout: An Expressive Arts Workbook for Healthcare Workers. 2021 CCHS Wellness Team. CCHS Wellness Playbook: Mindfulness, Yoga, Music and More. July 2021. She also facilitates healing ceremonies, workshops and rituals. You can find out more about her work at www.express-explore-expand.com www.expressiveartsmystery.net.

I CHOOSE FREEDOM

Suraya Susana Keating

If I were to write the way I breathe, if I were to write the way Mother Earth's heart beats, the way the wind sings, the waters flow, and fire dances, I would write with wild abandon—alive to the waters of words that long to pour through me. I'd feel the energy rise, letters shaping themselves into words, words into phrases, phrases into something moving through me, sourced from somewhere paradoxically beyond me and within me at the same time. Doors from and to infinity open as these words pour forth, swirling currents dancing through me as I surrender to the next wave, and the next, and the next.

There is no judgment. No comparison. No effort.

There is no need for my words to be grammatically correct, to make sense, or to be wrapped in a tidy bow. There is only the sensing within my body—the next impulse as it comes—and the embodiment of that impulse, expressed through words. Like tears tenderly caressing my cheek or the wild cry of my heart's eternal ache, I put my pen to the page and surrender to what is. To stop the flow would be a sin against my soul. To control the flow would be the petty work of my ego, that relentless competitor for space. But when I rest my heart on Mother Earth, I know, feel and trust beyond a shadow of a doubt that my words are an embodiment of her divine cycle of birth, death, rebirth - again and again and again.

The word that comes to me now is wild. Say it with me. Wild. Say it out loud. WILD. Sing it, shout it, whisper it. WILD. Wild is one of my favorite words—a reflection of my soul's longing to be free. It makes me want to press my heart to the Earth and sob like a newborn. To immerse my body in the ocean and wonder at the blanket of a billion stars above. To dance naked by a campfire, howling at the moon. To paint my face with mud, speak with my tree friends, and dig my hands into the soil so I can feel the earth beneath my nails.

I was born wild. We all were. But that wildness was quickly suppressed. Buried by layers of conditioning in a society that valued control, conformity and productivity over intuition, freedom and flow. Shaped by the programming I inherited from family, school, media, and culture—the endless script of what little girls should and should not be.

My parents were not allowed to be wild. And neither was I. As modeled by my mother and father, I learned at a young age to live in my head, not in my body or heart. I learned at a young age to worship cognitive intelligence over intuition. I was taught that higher education mattered much more than connection to my higher self. The mind was supreme, its logic a fortress against the untamed forces of emotion and instinct. In my family, intellect was the highest currency—far more valued than the body's wisdom, the heart's whispers, or the soul's quiet urgings.

I have compassion for my parents. They were only doing what they were taught, repeating the inherited trauma of a disconnected self. Little did they know, they had birthed a wild child, one who would break all their rules someday. You see, wildness cannot be held back forever. It is part of our design. It's like the sky trying to hold back a storm. At a certain point, the sky must surrender.

My life has been a reclaiming of my wild soul, the soul that is free and unfettered by social norms. A soul with a personality, one that fully inhabits its idiosyncratic quirks but also knows when to release the patterns of personality when the inner wolf comes a' howling.

During my first Saturn return, as layers of my outworn snakeskin began to shed, I enrolled in a year-long "Return to Your Wild Soul" training. We engaged in a vast array of practices designed to liberate us from the dominance of our logical minds, and focused on cultivating connection to our bodies, hearts, and intuition. We buried ourselves in the earth, forged friendships with trees, shed clothing to paint ourselves with mud, and breathed consciously into our three vital centers: the body, heart, and mind.

One particular moment of the "Return to Your Wild Soul" training stands out. On a beautiful sunny morning, my cohort and I decided to paint each others' naked bodies with mud. We dripped and smeared and anointed each others' bodies with mud until we began to resemble a raw, savage Jackson Pollock painting. We buried our legs in the earth up to our shins, forming a circle of bare bodies of all colors, shapes, and sizes, rooted in the soil like ancient trees. We abandoned words and spoke in sounds: howls, tones and melodies that wove together into an untamed symphony. For endless hours, we sang songs without words that only the body and soul could understand.

Submerged together in that primal womb of mud, we were no longer individuals: we were a tribe, a pulse, a living song - wild and free - woven back into the heartbeat of nature herself.

That moment of ecstatic expression with my forest kin was a turning point in my life. In that moment I fully remembered and embodied my inherent wildness.

It was as if I had finally returned home.

Now, when I feel disconnected from my wildness, I sometimes howl. At times the howl rises as a low, trembling whisper; other times, it erupts from my core in a fierce, untamed roar. However it emerges, the howl brings me home to myself—it reminds me of who I am and where I come from.

You see, wildness cannot be suppressed forever. It is part of our design. Like a storm pressing against the sky, it will not be contained. Sooner or later, the sky must break open. Wildness is a force within our bones, pulsing beneath our skin like a drumbeat in the dark.

My life has been a reclamation, an untethering of my wild soul. Every day, I am shedding the skin of who I was taught to be—peeling off the layers of politeness, perfection, and pleasing that never truly belonged to me. I release the scripts, the shoulds, the silent rules etched into my bones by a world afraid of untamed women. No more. I am stepping barefoot into the unknown, into the wind, into the fire of my own becoming. I am raw. I am wild. I am elemental. I howl not for permission but for liberation.

This is not a rebellion—it is a return.

During my first Saturn return, as the brittle layers of my past began to shed, I enrolled in a year-long "Return to Your Wild Soul" training. It was a passage back to my body, my instincts, my forgotten language. We engaged in practices that dismantled the tyranny of the logical mind and reawakened the dormant parts of ourselves. We buried ourselves in the earth, whispered secrets to trees, and breathed life into our three vital centers—body, heart, and mind. We shed the weight of fabric, smearing our skin with earth, remembering what it meant to belong.

One moment remains etched in my bones. My cohort and I stood together, naked and painted in mud, our hands gliding over skin like sculptors shaping clay. We buried our legs in the earth up to our shins, forming a sacred circle—bodies of all colors, shapes, and sizes, rooted in the soil like ancient trees. And then, something primal broke free. Words abandoned us. Instead, we spoke in sound—tones, howls, and melodies weaving together into a wild symphony. It was raw. It was untamed. A song beyond language, understood only by the body and soul.

In that moment, something shifted. I tasted my wildness fully, without apology. I was home.

I choose freedom.

BIOGRAPHY

SURAYA KEATING, MFT (#43996), REAT, RDT is a bilingual (Spanish-English) Registered Expressive Arts Therapist, Registered Drama Therapist, Clinical Supervisor and master trainer in Expressive Arts and Drama Therapy. Suraya played a key role in developing and expanding Marin Shakespeare's prison theater programs from a single prison (San Quentin) to 14 California prisons. She also co-founded Marin Shakespeare's Returned Citizens' Theater Troupe, a theater program for artists returning home from incarceration. She is an adjunct professor at the California Institute of Integral Studies, and former co-supervisor of an Expressive Arts Therapy Program at Contra Costa Health Services, where she provided training and supervision to MFT associates. Founder of Soul Story Theater, Suraya is passionate about the healing power of sharing our stories, and supports others in bringing forth meaningful true-life journeys and turning them into transformative solo performance pieces. Much of Suraya's 25 plus years of work in Expressive Arts and Drama Therapy has been in schools, prisons, hospitals as well as in private practice, and has focused on populations who are marginalized and oppressed. Suraya is also a proud mama, Playback Theater performer, actress, theater director, yogini, nature lover and wild soul at heart. www.suraya.org www.soulstorytheater.com www.expressiveartsmystery.net

PART 3
POETRY OF THE WILD

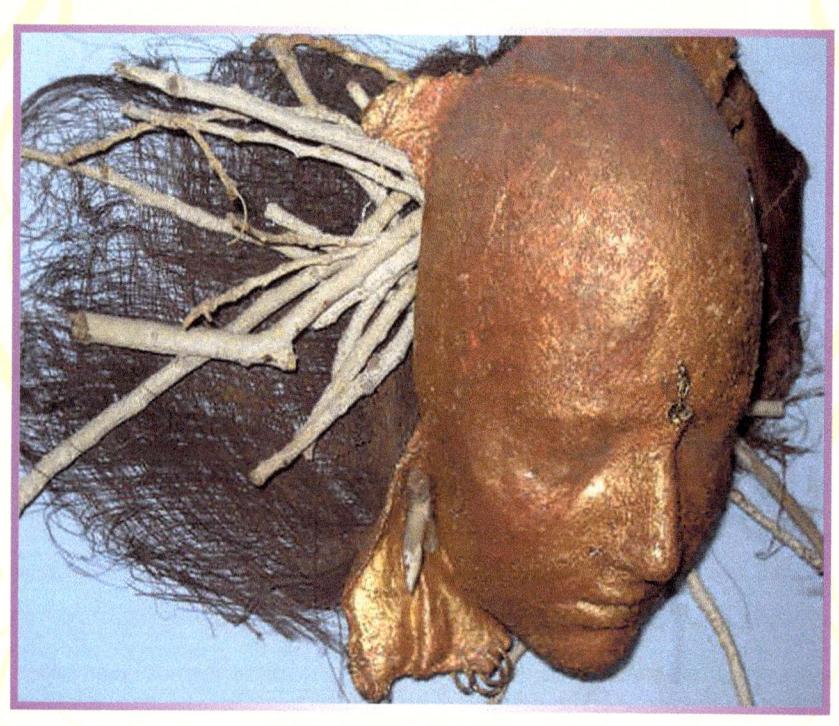

© Mireya Alejo Marcet

SAMILA – FROM SHAME TO BEAUTY

Mireya Alejo Marcet

I would like to begin this writing with a little story—one that serves to describe how my soul speaks to me, how art serves my life, and how the wild may be ignited to bring forth a fuller expression of who we are. With this, we continue opening our walk on this earth and the journey of the Soul. Hopefully, this telling will spark your own stories and journeys of insight, transformation, and the potency of trusting the language of our Soul to be expressed through the creative process.

A few years ago, I met someone who shook my world. It was one of those encounters that felt like a meeting of souls. Wanting to explore the depth of this connection, I took the initiative to get to know him better—something I had never done before. He accepted, and we met for coffee. It was a rich, flowing exchange, full of curiosity and resonance.

A few days later, I heard from a friend that he had gone back to his partner. He had let my friend know, as if to pass the message to me indirectly.

With this revelation, a deep well of shame rose within me—the kind of shame that arrives unbidden, spreading like a sticky residue in the body. The intensity of it was disproportionate to the situation, so I knew it held something far older, something deeper.

The very next day, I attended a two-day mask-making workshop. As I waited for my mask to dry, I sat in silence, my eyes closed. Images flooded my mind—visions of being buried alive, echoes of persecution. Some ancestral, some karmic, some tied to histories beyond my knowing.

When the mask was ready for painting, I followed an instinctive pull. I let my hands be my guide, smearing color onto the surface. Reds, browns, yellows—the shades of shame, fear, and rage. I covered it in sand, pressing my fingers into its contours, allowing all the emotions surging within me to be absorbed by the mask. I surrendered to the process, trusting the primal expression moving through my hands.

When the energy felt complete, I approached the banquet of materials laid out before me. I chose dried herbs lavender, roses, rosemary medicines to soothe the wounds held within the mask's form. Carefully, I nestled them inside its hollow, as if creating a bundle of protection, a sacred offering to the self that had carried this pain for lifetimes.

Then, it was time to adorn the front. As I searched through objects, two symbols called to me—a small image of Aphrodite and a fang. I also found branches, and as I placed the mask upon them, I learned they had been gathered in Death Valley. The synchronicity felt like a whisper from the unseen, affirming what my Soul already knew.

I left the workshop with a profound sense of peace and completion. Honored to have listened, grateful to have been guided. The process had reminded me of the field that awakens when we surrender to the language of the imaginal, how symbols, images, and feelings weave themselves into something sacred, turning raw material into beauty.

A few nights later, I had a dream. The mask appeared and spoke her name: Samila. As I drifted between sleep and waking, a poem poured through me. It came in Spanish, dictated from somewhere beyond, and later, I translated it into English.

SAMILA - DE LA VERGUENZA A LA BELLEZA
May 2024

Eres tu hermosa Afrodita?
Tu belleza emerge del encuentro mas profundo
de la verguenza fundida con la tierra.
Llegas ahora a abrirme nuevos caminos,
aquellos que embriagan al espiritu con el cuerpo.
Y al cuerpo con un grito de vida,
Vestida en oro ella te lleva en su centro como talisman,
El colmillo le entrega su alma guerrera,
Decorada, bella. Ella se muestra sin pena en la sensualidad eterna que su fuego devora,
Silenciosa aun, ella observa.
Eterno es el tiempo de las encarnaciones en donde ella fue silenciada,
oprimida, enterrada en vida,
Su despertar es lento, paulatino, cauteloso.
El pequeno viento de su respiracion sale por su boca en un susurro delicado,
Ella esta completamente presente ante el despertar de estas nuevas vibraciones,
Su cuerpo vibra cuando baila y sus poros sudan alegria y luz,
Ella descansa sobre el eterno femenino pues en esta entrega sabe que solo con ser, su fragancia riega a todos los que caminan a su lado.
Bella siempre seras pues tu exterior emana desde la luz del espiritu,
Danzas sin parar, sin importar que su mirada te reconozca,
Tu mirada ve hacia adentro, pues cualquier otra direccion es en vano.

SAMILA - FROM SHAME TO BEAUTY
May 2024

Is that you beautiful Aphrodite?
Your beauty emerges from the deepest encounter of shame merging with earth,
You arrive now to open new paths for me,
those which intoxicate the spirit with the body,
And the body with a cry of life,
Dressed in gold she carries you at her center as a talisman,
Her fang gives her her warrior soul,
Decorated, beautiful, she shows herself without shame in the eternal sensuality that her fire devours,
Still silent, she observes.
Eternal is the time of those incarnations she was silenced in,
oppressed, buried alive,
Her awakening is slow, gradual, cautious,
The little wind of her breath exhales through her mouth in a delicate whisper,
She is completely present as she witnesses the awakening of these new vibrations,
Her body explodes when she dances and her pores sweat with joy and light.
She rests in the eternal feminine, for in this surrender she knows that just by being,
her fragrance waters all who walk beside her.
You will always be beautiful because your exterior emanates from
the light of the spirit.
You dance without stopping, regardless of whether a gaze recognizes you,
Your gaze looks inward, because any other direction is in vain.

BIOGRAPHY

Mireya A. Marcet, MA. MFT, is a Mexican woman who has lived in California for the past 24 years and offers her work locally and internationally. She is an artist, expressive arts psychotherapist, Astrologer and Grof Holotropic Breathwork Facilitator and adjunct professor at CIIS.

She is the creator of "Altar Creation - A Canvas in Movement," a practice that offers diverse applications to connect with our interior life and the sacred through the creation of altars and a multimodal integration with them. She offers regular women's expressive arts circles and courses in Integration of expanded states of consciousnes, weaving Holotropic Breathwork, expressive arts, sacred practices, somatic mindfulness and work with the natural world.

Mireya genuinely thrives in the unknown and trusts the transformative potential of the creative process. Because she continually turns to the arts for healing in her own life, her clients find it safe to explore, uncover, and release from the depths of the psyche. She offers online and in person individual psychotherapy & group sessions, consultation and teaching in Grass Valley, CA, Bay Area and Mexico. Her website: www.almaquecanta.com

JOURNEY TO DEEP SOVEREIGNTY

Aimee Tomczak

© Aimee Tomczak - Original acrylic painting (30" x 40")

On her journey, she has learned to descend into her deep earth soul, embracing the heavier emotional spaces she once avoided. Her paintbrush becomes a conduit, coaxing hidden emotions from the depths of her psyche—feelings long suppressed in the pursuit of comfort and the avoidance of pain.

With presence and creative courage, she has discovered how to express, listen to, and trust these emotions as integral parts of herself—acknowledging them without allowing them to define her vast wholeness. Colors swirl on the canvas, tenderly carrying difficult emotions. She allows creativity to flow, a river of expression and healing. Water moves with her memories, awakening hidden jewels that rise in spirals of recognition. Her true nature and essence emerge through these moments of bittersweet loss.

She is not alone. Lioness, her soul companion and guide, appeared first in a dream. At first, she hesitated, afraid to let Lioness in—fearful of the immense power of this animal companion who had been calling out to her, waiting with patient persistence. It was only when she broke free from her own cage that she could allow her inner wild divine to come forth and play.

Now, with Lioness by her side, she understands how the cosmos aligns with essential energy through her divine line—the sacred connection between sun, moon, and earth. She feels the veins of earthy energy pulsing beneath her feet, the rivers flowing in harmony with her awakened vision. The beauty and complexity of humans, of herself, unfold before her eyes.

Playful energies of pleasure and wild joy dance with her deep inner knowing. She senses the layered intelligence of the right and left brain, woven into the cosmic rhythm. She awakens to her own light—the shimmering life force that pulses through everything. Hope swells within her as she allows her heart to be cradled by the wise earth knowing, the sustaining force of life on this extraordinary planet.

Her heart opens to the tender reeds of the vast earth, where intellect and spirit entwine. Right and left brain move together, a cosmic dance of energy, drawing her deeper into the universal intelligence that breathes within every living form.

Gratitude fills her being—an unshakable reverence for this journey, for the profound experience of connection, sovereignty, and belonging.

May we all know this connection. May all beings be sovereign, alive, and creatively wild and free.

BIOGRAPHY

Aimee Tomczak, LMFT, is licensed psychotherapist, Artist, and Certified Intentional Creativity Coach / Painting facilitator from Musea Institute. She has been using Expressive Arts and embodiment for healing with people of all walks of life for two decades. With a background as a dancer, performer/actress and artist, creative expression has always been life sustaining.

However, after a Midlife crisis/ Awakening and not painting for 19 years, Aimee picked up the paintbrush again in 2020 - which literally saved and rebirthed her life.

Her artwork can be seen at Fulton Crossing Gallery in Sonoma County, Art at the Source Open Studios 2024, and online. She leads Intentional Creativity workshops at Fulton Crossing Gallery and also offers 1:1 sessions using Creativity for healing.

Aimee brings a heartfelt presence, playful compassion and depth and has been called a "Creative Catalyst" by many.

See her artwork here:

https://www.aimeetomczakart.com and ttps://www.fultoncrossing.com

Info on her offerings and healing work: https:// www.aimeetomczak.com/

INNER WILD

© Nicki Koethner

THE ESSENCE OF MY SOUL
SACRED OBJECTS: LOST AND FOUND
Nicki Koethner

When I look at childhood pictures of mine,
I'm looking to connect to the essence of my spirit:
My soul in the midst of the larger soul: the universe.
Memories and stories emerging constantly unfolding:
Put together in a piece seen and unseen.

What did I know then that I have forgotten?
Who was I? Who am I now?
What is the essence that shines through?

For me, it is going back to the source:
To connect with the red thread of my being,
My core, unperturbed by social conditioning.
Simply being in my being.

Creating the piece is engaging with myself:
honoring the gifts, opening to the essence of myself
within the larger mystery of life and the universe.

My aunt, who is no longer alive,
sent me this picture years ago, saying she still sees this look in me today.
What do I see when I look at this picture?

A sleepy-looking straight-forwardness, sadness, clarity and a strong will.
Relaxed and *sincere* are other qualities evoked in me.
The hand in a fist- legs spread out, open.
There is a certain serenity in it all.

Bird-feathers,
Raven, owl, turkey, pigeon and geese
Shells and stones, wood and moss,
Soil and roots,
Clay-figures,
Elements - me within them- part of them- being them.

INNER WILD

I'm part of the universe. Unique and not so unique.
Placed in the interconnectedness of everything.
What I know is what I feel
What I experience…
This is the uniqueness that I can share with the world.
What do you see and feel?
I hope it inspires your own story,
and connection with the essence of you.

> **Prompts:** Pick a childhood picture of yours and start dialoguing with it. Collect items in nature that you feel drawn to and that have colors that you love, and create a collage with your childhood picture to honor the essence of you. The following questions might guide you to interact on a deeper level with the essence of your soul and also touch upon ways your childhood experiences distorted that essence.
>
> - What would you like me to know?
> - How do you feel? Is there a story you like to tell me?
> - What is the essence of you that I might have forgotten?
> - See if memories emerge whether joyful or painful. Is there anything that is needed for the child to be heard and seen in new ways?
> - Do you connect with parts that have been forgotten and want to be recovered and re-invited into your life?

MESSAGE FROM WATER
Suraya Susana Keating

I am Water.
I am the pulse beneath the skin of the world.
I feel everything—like silk soaked in memory.
I move through all things, a liquid whisper
slipping through the cracks of resistance.
I let the world shape me—
a mirror, a womb, a storm.

As Creek,
I ribbon down the mountain's spine,
a silver serpent weaving between bones of stone.
I flirt with gravity,
curling around the knuckles of boulders,
brushing the hair of wind-blown grasses.
I zigzag through the earth's moods,
each bend a prayer, each turn a trust fall
into the arms of the unknown.

As River,
I pour through tree-lined valleys
Easing my way around ancient stones
Colorful meadows and farmlands
Nourishing and purifying
All that lives within me
And all that lives around me.
I am the bloodstream of the land—carrying memory,
Cleansing sorrow, feeding song.

INNER WILD

As Ocean,
I am the womb of the world—vast, ancient, unknowable.
I flirt with the edges of certainty,
Kissing the sand with a lover's patience
Then slipping away into mystery.
Each wave a breath—I ebb and flow—
I touch and retreat, greet and release,
Forever dancing with the edge of becoming.

As Mist,
I rise like a secret prayer, unseen but felt,
Departing Mother for a time.
The Earth exhales and I ascend—
A soft letting go, a trust fall into sky.
I am the ghost of water,
Floating toward the unknown
Until I clothe myself in clouds
And become sky-dancer, shape-shifter, dream-weaver.

As Rain or Snow,
I fall like blessings from the unseen—
Diamond tears, showers of grace, crysts of truth.
Each drop a messenger,
Each snowflake a sacred syllable.
I kiss rooftops, rivers, faces, soil—
And awaken life wherever I land.
I fall down unapologetically,
Blessing the sky and earth with
My mighty purifying power.

And the cycle begins anew.

INNER WILD

As Water,
I am the great Rememberer.
There is nothing I cannot slip past, wear down, or become.
When life sets stone in my path,
I do not resist.
I curve, caress, and flow.
I do not fear the mountain—I carve it.
I do not name the block—I bless it.
In every collision, I find communion.
What others call obstacle,
I call partner,
And together,
We create a new way forward.

Part 4

VOICES OF THE ELDERS

INTRODUCTION BY SURAYA KEATING

To me, elders hold in their eyes an expression of the timeless love of their heart and soul. Through enduring many seasons, and weathering many joys and storms, elders offer us a unique perspective that is shaped by years of raw life experience. Not only have many elders been through their own trials and tribulations personally, but many have also witnessed the world in its rise and fall. Many have found peace in nature, and in life's shifting forms.

I remember my Ukrainian-born grandmother, Millie, who for much of her life carried a heaviness from trauma that expressed itself mostly through bitterness at others and attempts to control. However, when my grandmother passed through the portal of her 90th year on the planet, something magical happened. Whatever metaphorical bags of rocks she was carrying started to melt away. A brightness came back to her eyes and a calmness to her heart. My grandmother began finding humor in everything, and began laughing at herself frequently.

As my grandmother moved through her nineties, her cognitive functioning declined rapidly in memory, sharpness and use of words. But quite gracefully and without any apparent effort on her part, Grandma's heart began to blossom.

An avid birder in her younger years, grandma used to sit on the deck of her 21st floor apartment in Manhattan and point out details of every kind of bird she saw to my brothers and I. As she moved into her later years, those details were forgotten, but her connection to the birds seemed to grow stronger. Instead of identifying the birds by name and explaining them in a logical way, Grandma began singing to the birds – letting bird sounds pour out from her chest with wild abandon. To me, Grandma was connecting with these wild creatures in the most simple and profound way.

While I was unfortunately not present when Grandma transitioned to the spirit world at age 99 in the nursing home where she was living, it was said that she died with a smile on her face.

This short story about my grandmother makes me think about how there are certain lessons in life that only age and experience can bestow. Grandma moved through the heartache and trauma of her life in her own way. In the end, she became pure in her soul and deeply connected to the bird creatures that were, perhaps, a kind of spirit guide for her.

In this section, we highlight the voices of elders as a way to honor the key role of elders as guardians of a flavor of wisdom that only comes through ripening. The perspectives of elders offer unique and invaluable insights related to human's relationship to the wild. Having lived through many changing landscapes, internally and externally, elders serve as beacons that can guide future generations.

May the voices of elders help set us free.

UNEARTHING THE UNDERWORLD WOMB TEMPLE
Kerani Marie

From before my birth
The Great Mother Archetype
The Womb and
The Wound
Were woven into
The fabric of my existence

Culture minimized my innate
Connection to the natural world
Disregarding my soulful being
Cutting my archetypal threads
From the roots of my primal mother

Molded to fit in I shrunk and dried up
Beauty and appearance came before the soul
Guilt and shame overrode being wild and free

Shrinking and acting the part
Ate away at my life force
Conforming and wanting to be loved
Overrode my innate knowing

When my womb was impregnated at 17
Alcohol was the river of consciousness
When my womb was slugged by the baby's father
Hoping it would start my period
When an aunt created a concoction
Hoping after I drank it, I would abort
I felt small and betrayed

INNER WILD

Guilty and filled with shame
Confused, conflicted, and lost

My mother asked why would I have sex,
Telling me I had to marry in a pink dress
Telling me to hold my stomach in
On my wedding day
Walking down the aisle the voice in my head
Yelling, I'm not a bad girl

Sixty years after my son's birth
And 50 years of spiritual and emotional healing
Cultivating a connection to the natural world
Exploring my divine feminine essence
Trusting my innate intuition and soulful life
I was called to build a womb temple
The primal mother and archetypal energies
Were clear, potent, and permeated my being

Grace and visions flooded my world
Inspiration, creativity, and listening led my way
The Divine Masculine showed up creating the structure
I remained open to what wanted to be born
Listening and feeling into how I would
Open a portal to this sacred space

Humbled and filled with respect for this honor
The grace-filled vision was manifest
Nine months from inception to creation
With the shared wisdom of seven birth doulas
The Underworld Womb temple was consecrated

A week before the consecration of the womb
I had a sense of karmic change entering the field
It was revealed when my son's father

INNER WILD

Passed from this worldly plane just
Two days after the womb's consecration
A complete circle of life and death
Danced in the womb cycle of creation

After many ceremonies in the womb temple
Through the tears, prayers, gratitude, howls, drums,
songs, surrendering and celebrations
I was awakened into my own embodied truth
The womb temple was built to heal my womb
The wombs of all women and the hearts of men
The Womb was to be honored and receive offerings
For her Soulful, Wild, Iconic Expression
Alive within her creation portal
The primal mother's infinite potential
Offers herself as a spiritual friend.

The Underworld Womb Temple
My offering for deeply healing
the feminine and masculine energies
Forward and back in time
To remember who we are and
To stand in the wholeness of love
Embracing all aspects of being human
Spirit, matter, and energy, dancing and weaving life
I humbly stand in grace
Tempered by the fire
Of the womb cauldron
Bowing to the mystery of
The Underworld Womb Temple
1/14/24

BIOGRAPHY

Kerani Marie is a Soulful Inner Wisdom Guide for women on the sacred feminine journey. She is also a Creative Muse for bringing your story and art to Life. With over 45 years of immersion in multicultural spiritual teachings and healing practices, her wisdom is informed by direct experience with spiritual and healing crises and the emerging into wholeness and freedom.

Kerani Marie is an Artist and Author. Her authentic heart inspires the conscious emergence of souls through her writings, art, ceremonies, and rituals. She is also a Craniosacral Practitioner and Reiki Master.

Kerani Marie is the founder of The Underworld Womb Temple, The Center for Living Wisdom, The Soulgazm Rendezvous, and Romancing Grief - Alchemy of Heartbreak. She is the author of Emerging Woman, A Rite of Passage from Shame to Freedom and The Cycle of Life Journey. She lives in Sedona, AZ.

GOING OUT AND RETURNING WITH MY GIFTS FOR MY PEOPLE

Sharon Reinbott

"There is only one life you can call your own and a thousand others you can call by any name you want."
David Whyte, "All the True Vows"

When you go out in the woods, out into the desert; when you climb to the mountaintop, or sit by a stream and fast and pray – things happen. And if you are lucky, you return bearing a gift for your people: the gift of your true self, the gift of knowing your name.

Ten years ago, I performed a Vision Fast in the wilderness of Death Valley, California, severing me from my old life, old career, and destroyed marriage. Before my solitary fast, my reasons for being there were scrutinized by skilled guides. They demanded, *"Are you an Elder?"* and dared me to claim my Elderhood. When I said I wanted to manifest my gifts, they demanded, *"What are your gifts?"* They pushed and cajoled me into making my statement, so I knew why I was going out there.

I am an Elder who has thrown off the chains that bind her. I claim my gifts of Charisma, Wildness, Radiance, Insight, Wisdom and Joy, and I dare to manifest them in the world.

They would not rest until I had used the word "dare." They wanted its juice. *My* juiciness.

At daybreak, they awakened me with a cup of tea, prayed over me, and blessed me. I shouldered my pack and went off to spend four days and nights in solitude, fasting on the valley floor. There was no human company, no structure of a day around meals, no human to hear me scream – or sing. No person, group or institution to judge me, love me, or set the rules. There, were the sky, the ravens, the rocks, the creosote, and the mountains for my company and my teachers. There was Presence all around me.

At night I slept under the stars, watching Orion make his way around Polaris, to guess how much of the night had passed. My senses were heightened, and I knew that the wilderness sensed me. It was unnerving. But in that solitude, the fabricated persona I had so carefully built for over 60 years began to fall apart.

I claimed the Earth as my mother, and She claimed me as her daughter. Together, we rid the abusive men from my heart. In the vulnerability of a solitary life away from the collective, I embraced my gifts, and I became *fierce*.

On the morning after the fourth night, when the sun crested the mountain, I returned, bearing my gifts. The ravens followed me, attending the ceremony in which I told my story.

I entered the wilderness as one person, and emerged as another, a truer self, having made a promise it would kill me to break.

I went out into the wilderness, and my life began. I am part of the Great Story. I am who I am.

BIOGRAPHY

Sharon Reinbott (M.A) is a hymnist and lay theologian. At retirement from a successful career, she headed to Death Valley to perform a Vision Fast, daring to name her soul gifts and offer them to the world. She received her M.A. in Culture and Spirituality from the Sophia Center at Holy Names University in Oakland, CA, where her work concentrated on the rewriting of Christian hymns to help bring about what

Fr. Thomas Berry, CP described as a more beneficial relationship of the human to the earth.

She brings to her work a mixture of deep wisdom, creative thinking, and a wild, untamed, and fierce spirit, along with the thinking of Thomas Berry, Pierre Teilhard de Chardin, Bill Plotkin, and Clarissa Pinkola Estés. Years of practice of archetypal dream work have taught her to feel into the dream images, deepening her own spiritual work. Her practice of Biodanza since 2005 has deepened her ability to be truly present with another. She fervently believes that, with images that provide an increased understanding of human relationship to the evolution of the Universe, we can sing our way into its story.

REFLECTIONS
Saunterre Irish

Thank you for offering me the opportunity to contribute to your book. I've never felt as though I have any elder wisdom to offer and have mostly felt like a learner. When I was a member of a lesbian feminist clergy group, the others who were younger than I taught me quite a bit. Now I'm feeling my way as a 74-year-old trans man who stopped testosterone about 5 years ago realizing my body was going to do whatever it was going to do as an aging human being! Very disappointing I must say!! So, I'm slowly inhabiting Thich Nhat Hanh's Five Remembrances:

- "I am of the nature to grow old. There is no way to escape growing old.
- I am of the nature to have ill health. There is no way to escape ill health.
- I am of the nature to die. There is no way to escape death. All that is dear to me and everyone I love are of the nature to change.
- There is no way to escape being separated from them.
- My actions are my only true belongings. I cannot escape the consequences of my actions. My actions are the ground upon which I stand."

For the first time in my life, I'm being treated by a traditional Chinese 5-Element Acupuncturist and receiving that wisdom medicine. Found Eliot Cowan's Plant Spirit Medicine book and being enlightened by his wondrous experience and wisdom in relationship with the spirits of plants.

I think my body heart mind is being opened in ways to what Mother Earth has been offering all along that I'd not previously been aware was possible! I'm grateful to be receiving so much as an elder!

BIOGRAPHY

A favorite photo of mine circa 1953 shows a 3- or 4-year-old me sitting on my dark red and white metal tricycle that had a fender over the front wheel. I'm wearing a snowsuit with mittens attached to my cuffs with clips. I feel ready to go off on an imaginary adventure.

My dad's transfer to Paris in 1965 sent me to the American School of Paris located in Madame du Barry's mansion for my sophomore year of high school. In 1979 I married a man. In 2019 I married a woman. Before and in-between I worked at a secretarial school, then for a doctor, then a vet, a short 2-summer stint as an Air Force Chaplain candidate, officiated at traditional and same-sex weddings, ran a cottage rental business on Lake Michigan, designed a log home, finished the interior in wood, and lived on a sheep farm in VT for 3 years. In 2007 I transitioned FTM. Suddenly the little child in the snowsuit on the tricycle became the gender expression I knew was inside all along.

All an adventure I didn't plan but for which I am immensely grateful. Now Molly and I are living in Berkeley, CA, with weekly hikes in Point Reyes National Seashore mixed with long walks in San Francisco. That yearning for adventure in the simplicity of a tricycle and snowsuit with mittens I can't lose is still alive and well in my 74-year-old body mind spirit.

PART 5

PRACTICES

Do you love creativity, play and nature as much as we do? If so, we hope that this chapter will tickle your inner muse and awaken your wild soul. We offer a rainbow of expressive arts practices for you to engage with, organized and inspired by the four elements of Earth, Water, Fire & Air, plus a category we call "Mixed Elements Practices." Each practice intentionally interweaves the arts with nature to promote connection to yourself and to the elements within you and all around you. As with any suggested exercises, feel free to intuitively change and adapt these activities according to your own soul's guidance. With these practices, we hope to offer you an array of powerful ways to connect with your soul, shift mood states, access wisdom, and bring you more deeply into your bodies and hearts.

EARTH PRACTICES

The miracle is not to fly in the air or walk on water,
but to walk on the earth.

-Chinese Proverb

The blurry image in this photograph speaks to the transitory nature
of our being on Earth, and to the illusion of our separateness.

MESSAGES FROM THE EARTH

Materials: Pen and paper (optional: coloring or painting materials)

Instructions:

- Sit or lie down somewhere in nature.
- Take a few minutes to sense your body and breath.
- Scan the environment and notice if there is part of nature, such as a particular tree, rock, body of water, cloud, etc., that you feel drawn to.
- Once you have identified a part of nature that you feel drawn to, greet this part of nature in any way that feels right to you. For example, say hello to a tree and genuinely thank the tree for its presence.
- Next, ask the part of nature you have chosen if it has any messages or guidance for you. When you feel inspired, pick up your pen and write down any messages that wish to come through.

Adaptations: In addition to writing down messages, draw the part of nature that you are drawn to in your journal. Alternatively, instead of writing down messages verbally, draw or paint whatever wants to emerge.

NATURE SCULPTURES

Materials: Rocks, fallen leaves, sticks, feathers, shells, sand, dirt and anything you can find from nature that feels in integrity to use

Instructions:

- Take time to sit or lie down in nature somewhere. Connect to your breath and body. Invite in a sense of connection to the body and breath of the land you are sitting or lying down on.

- Open your eyes and notice any natural objects you feel drawn to. Gather objects and begin to create an intuitive sculpture with those objects in any way that you are guided.
- Once your nature sculpture feels complete, sit with the sculpture and see if it has any messages for you.

Adaptations: This is a lovely practice to do in silence with a buddy, or even with a small group. Allow the sculpture to evolve naturally without planning or controlling the process.

MULTIPLE SENSES POETRY

Instructions:

- Choose a place in nature that you love.
- Sit down and notice what arises in your five senses. Ask yourself:
- What do I see? Write down a few words about what you see.
- What do I hear? Write down a few words about what you hear.
- What do I smell? Write down a few words about what you smell.
- What do I feel? Write down a few lines about textures you're aware of or what you feel inside?
- What do I taste? Write down what you imagine this landscape tastes like.
- What do I imagine? Write down anything that this landscape inspires in your imagination.

Using the words you wrote down for inspiration, write a 6-line poem using the following structure:

I SEE _____
I HEAR _____
I SMELL _____
I TASTE _____

INNER WILD

I FEEL _____
I IMAGINE _____

Adaptations: Instead of being in nature, you can gaze at an image of nature or use your imagination to invoke a scene from nature to do this writing practice.

Start writing, no matter what.
The water does not flow unless the faucet is turned on.
-Louis L'Amour

"I AM" POEMS

Materials: Pen and paper (optional: coloring or painting materials)

Instructions:

- Sit down in a garden or anywhere outside. Alternatively, if the weather does not permit sitting outside, look out a window where there is a view that is pleasing to you.
- As you look around you, write down at least 9 things you see or hear that are pleasing or inspiring to you. Add any details you wish to what you write down. For example, you might write down words such as: pink sky at sunrise, leaves sparkling with light, squirrels climbing sunflower in bloom birds singing their morning song, the wind, children laughing, green moss, a willow tree

Next, take a piece of paper and write down the words "I am" as a sentence starter for 4 separate lines

- I am -
- I am -
- I am -
- I am -

INNER WILD

Create an "I am" poem by filling in the four "I am" prompts with whatever words you wish of what you have written down. Feel free to change or add any words that come to you intuitively. Here is an example of an "I am" poem inspired by the words listed above:

- I am the bluebird singing her morning song.
- I am the pink sky of new possibility at sunrise.
- I am the sunflower blooming and fading and blooming again.
- I am leaves sparkling with the light of peace.

When finished, share your poem aloud to yourself or share with someone you feel comfortable sharing around

Adaptations: If this practice is done with a buddy or in groups, have participants swap poems when comfortable and have partners read participants' poems back to them, changing "I" to "you" to serve as affirmations.

EARTH DANCING

Materials: None but a patch of land that you feel connected to, or would like to feel more connected to.

Instructions:

- Find a patch of land that you feel connected to, or would like to feel more connected to. If possible, remove your shoes and stand or walk barefoot on this land. Greet and thank the land in whatever way feels right to you.
- Next, begin to imagine that everything around you is your dance partner. If there is a tree, let the tree be your dance partner. If there is a rock, let the rock be your dance partner. Play, move and dance with the Earth in whatever way you feel inspired.

- Let the Earth dance with you. Invite a small shift in your awareness such that you are not the one doing the dancing, but rather the Earth is dancing with you. Notice what happens.

Adaptations: Earth dancing can be done with a partner or small group.

ROCK DRUMMING

Materials: A few rocks of different sizes

Instructions:

- Gather a few rocks of different sizes.
- Explore the sounds each rock makes against the other rocks.
- Choose some rocks to be "drums" and 1-2 other rocks to be the "drum sticks.".
- Begin creating your own rhythm by "drumming" on the rocks.
- If you are with friends, they can join in on their own rocks to create a drum jam together.

WATER PRACTICES

If there is magic on this planet, it is contained in water.
-Loren Eiseley

WATER DANCING

- Place: A body of water which you can dip your feet or legs into or immerse yourself in more completely.

Instructions:

- Step into a body of water (river, ocean, creek, etc.). Sense your body and breath. Sense the aliveness of the water around you.
- Next, begin to imagine that the water is your dance partner. Play, move and dance with the water in whatever way you feel inspired.

- Let the water dance with you. Invite a small shift in your awareness such that you are not the one doing the dancing, but rather the water is dancing with you. Notice what happens.

ADAPTATIONS: Water dancing can be done with a partner or with a small group.

I found I could say things with color and shapes
That I couldn't say any other way - things I had no words for.
-Georgia O'Keeffe

WATER GUIDANCE ART & JOURNALING

Materials: Paper, pen, colored pencils, pastels, watercolors, oil paints, etc.

Instructions

- Find a river, creek, ocean or other body of water, or simply imagine that you are by a river, creek, ocean or other body of water. Then, sit or lie down in a comfortable position.
- Take a few minutes to sense your body and breath and sense into the sound of the water flowing.
- Invite a connection to the wisdom of the body of water you are near (or imagined body of water) by asking:
  - "What do you - water - want me to know?"
  - "In what ways does my life want to flow at this moment in time?"
  - "What wisdom or guidance wants to flow through me?"
- When you feel inspired, write anything down in your journal that you feel the river (or water in any form) wants to communicate.
- Next, create an image through drawing, watercolor, oil pastels, etc. that expresses the guidance you have received.

- Finally, sit with your words and image and see what arises. If you wish, pick up your pen and write down any additional messages that wish to come through.

ADAPTATIONS: In addition to drawing, painting and/or writing down messages, you are also welcome to sing, dance or express messages in whatever way that feels true to you.

***

GRIEF RITUAL

Materials: Journal, pieces of organic paper, pen, pencil

Instructions:

- Go to a river or creek with flowing water.
- Sit down by the river and write about whatever you are in grief about, or who or what you are grieving. If you feel drawn, you might write respond to the prompts:
    - My heart is full of grief for…
    - I am grateful for….
    - I now choose to release….
- Notice your feelings and write about them if you wish.
- With organic pencils, write down on small strips of organic paper or on fallen leaves whatever it is you wish to let go of.
- Release your strips of paper or the fallen leaves into the river one at a time. Let yourself be as spacious as you wish in contemplating what it feels like to let go.
- Practice gratitude for all that arises.
- Finish by sitting in meditation, or by singing a song of your choice that nourishes your heart.

FIRE PRACTICES

Set your life on fire. Seek those who fan your flames.

-Rumi

FLAME GAZING

Materials: A candle, fireplace with fire or an outdoor campfire.

Instructions:

- Light a candle or a fire in a fireplace or in an outdoor campfire.
- Sit and gaze at the flame for 15-30 minutes.
- Notice what feelings, sensations, thoughts, memories or images arise.

FIRE GUIDANCE ART & JOURNALING

Materials: A candle, fireplace with fire or an outdoor campfire. Paper, pen, colored pencils, pastels, watercolors, oil paints, etc.

Instructions

- Light a candle or a fire in a fireplace or in an outdoor campfire. Then, sit down and be with the fire.
- Take a few minutes to sense your body and breath and sense into the image, sounds and heat of the fire.
- Invite a connection to the wisdom of fire (or imagined fire) by asking:
- "What do you - fire - want me to know? What guidance do you have for me?"
- "What wants to be burned away or released from my life at this moment in time?"
- "What am I passionate about?"

RELEASE AND LETTING GO

Materials: Find small wooden sticks on a walk (popsicle sticks or toothpicks work well too). Candle, matches or lighter. Bowl.

Instructions:

- Take deep breaths and hold sticks in your hands connecting with something that you are ready to release. It might be something like self-limiting beliefs, identities you have held on to, feelings of anger and resentment, or anything that no longer serves you.
- Pick one per stick and one for each sitting. You can make it a daily or weekly practice. Make sure you are connected with the energy and feeling before burning the stick.

- Burn the stick in a candle flame or with a lighter and watch the burning and discard in a bowl so you do not burn yourself. Connect with the energy of release. Take another deep breath, place your hand on your heart and make any sound after the ritual is complete.

AIR PRACTICES

That's life: starting over, one breath at a time.

—Sharon Salzberg

IMPROVISED SOUNDS, HUMMING AND YOUR BODY AS DRUM

Materials: Your body, voice and sounds inside and outside of you. This is an effective method to change inner dialogue, especially inner critic voices or the heaviness of repeated mental stories.

Instructions:

- Allow yourself to make any sounds with your voice and simply play around with sounds. Play around with volume and pitch and add movement to it.

- You could start by just vocalizing simple sounds, such as the vowels (a, e, i, o, u) or playful phrases like "blah blah" or "lalala," and let your creativity guide you.
- The sounds could also be mimicking the sounds of animals, nature, or even everyday background noises like a heater or the drip of water from a faucet. Turn this into a fun game, especially while hiking or walking, as you discover new sonic textures around you.
- Humming is another way of changing the frequency and vibrancy in our bodies. Humming has the potential to move blocked energy and to shift energy when we are caught in our minds.
- Play with others by sending sounds to each other and imitating each other's sounds.

YOUR BODY AS INSTRUMENT

Materials: Your body, voice and sounds inside and outside of you.
Instructions:

- Use your body as a drum or instrument when you wake up in the morning. Use your hands to drum up and down your body to activate all the cells in your body.
- Use your belly and hands to make a beautiful percussion sound. Clap your hands rhythmically to a count of 1-2 and then on your legs, play with frequency and sequence.
- Use your index finger to make a blop sound with your mouth by blowing up your cheeks, inserting the finger and letting it blop. Whistle and find other ways to improvise using your body as an instrument.

Music expresses that which cannot be put into words
And that which cannot remain silent

-Victor Hugo

LULLABIES TO SELF

Materials: Your body & voice.

Instructions:

- Sing yourself a lullaby by placing your hand on your heart, feeling the vibration of the sound: "*I love you and I'm with you - you are never alone.*"
- Make up your own lines that help you to soothe yourself and your nervous system to enhance self-love and compassion.

MIXED ELEMENTS PRACTICES

*A great silent space holds all of nature
in its embrace. It also holds you.*

-Eckhart Tolle

CREATE AN ELEMENTAL PLAYLIST

Materials: A device that plays music where you can make a playlist

Instructions:

- Reflect on songs that connect you to the elements of Earth, Water, Fire and Air, or to any elements you feel drawn to.
- Create an "elemental playlist" in which you choose at least two songs to represent each element.
- Listen to your "elemental playlist" to support your connection to the elements. Alternatively, if you feel in need of medicine from one particular element, you can focus on songs that represent that element.

Adaptations: Feel free to use the Elemental Playlist you create for the Elemental Movement practice described next.

Dance is the hidden language of the soul of the body.

-Martha Graham

ELEMENTAL MOVEMENT

Place: Any place outside or inside that feels safe and inviting.

Materials (optional): Music that inspires various elements of earth, water, fire and air. *You may also use the "Elemental Playlist" activity described in the MUSIC section to accompany this activity.

Instructions:

- In this activity, you are invited to move your body in ways that are inspired by the four elements of earth, water, fire and air. If there is a different elemental frame you wish to use (such as the five elements of earth, water, fire, air and space), please do what intuitively feels right to you.
- If you wish to use music, choose a song, or songs, that embody earth element. Call in and visualize earth element, and then let your body move as if earth element is moving through you.
- Repeat with water, fire and air elements.
- After air element, sit in meditation for 10 minutes or longer. Notice what is alive in you.

Adaptations: After the meditation, feel free to journal, write poetry or create art with any medium that calls you.

All you need in the world is love and laughter.
To have love in one hand and laughter in the other. That's all you need.

-August Wilson

ELEMENTAL CHARACTERS

Materials: Fabrics, leaves, sticks, costume items

Instructions:

- Connect to an element of nature that you would like to dress up as for a day. For example, you could choose to be a character named Earth, Water, Fire or Air.
- After you have chosen your character, adorn yourself in whatever way you wish.
- Go out into nature with a friend or friends who are also dressed up as an element, and embody this element as you play in nature together.

THEME-INSPIRED NATURE ALTARS

Materials: Rocks, fallen leaves, sticks, feathers, shells, sand, dirt and anything you can find in nature that feels in integrity to use

Instructions:

- Take time to sit or lie down in nature somewhere. Connect to your breath and body. Invite in a sense of connection to the body and breath of the land you are sitting or lying down on.
- Next, ask yourself: "What is a quality or energy that would be helpful to bring forth in my life at this moment?" For example, it may be of benefit to cultivate acceptance, compassion, courage, self-love or something else. Collect items in nature that you feel drawn to and that have colors that you love, and create a collage with your childhood picture to honor the essence of you.
- Once you have clarity around the quality or energy you wish to cultivate, begin to intuitively create an altar, using objects from nature.

Adaptations: This activity can be done with a partner or small group. Allow the sculpture to evolve naturally without planning or controlling the process.

GRATITUDE RITUAL

Materials: Journal or paper, pen, pencil

Instructions:

- Go to a favorite outdoor location.
- Sit down and reflect on whatever you are grateful for. If you feel drawn, you might write respond to the prompts:
    - I am grateful for….
    - My heart is full of gratitude for…
- Something challenging in my life that I choose to be grateful for is…
- Write down in your journal or on paper whatever you are grateful for.
- Notice your feelings and write about them if you wish.
- Finish by sitting in meditation, or by singing a song about gratitude, or a song of your choice that feels nourishing to you.

EDITOR'S BIO

Nicki Koethner & Suraya Keating

Co-creators of the Expressive Arts Mystery School and of this Inner Wild book, we are two friends and creative collaborators who met years ago, discovering our shared mission to heal through art, dance, and community. We have danced and worked together, creating spaces for others to find their voice and connect to their hearts. Inner Wild grew from the lived experience that creative expression is a pathway to healing. (www.expressiveartsmystery.net)

We invited friends and colleagues to contribute to this book as a tribute to the power of our shared humanity and the wisdom of the earth. We hope you find something in these pages that ignites your soul and helps you remember that we are all, at our core, a part of nature, wild and full of love.

www.ingramcontent.com/pod-product-compliance
Ingram Content Group UK Ltd.
Pitfield, Milton Keynes, MK11 3LW, UK
UKHW022122230426
12048UKWH00011BA/661